Mathete
Email: publishin

GOLF
GLEANINGS

Written and illustrated by
G. E. Stevens.

ISBN: 978-1-9196180-3-6

First Published in England (in 2021) by:
Mathetes Publishing,

Printed in Great Britain for Mathetes Publishing by Printondemand-
worldwide, 9, Culley Court, Bakewell Rd., Orton Southgate, PE2 5BJ

GOLF GLEANINGS

Written and illustrated by G. E. Stevens.

CONTENTS.

GOLF GLEANINGS.

And whatever you do, do *it* <u>heartily</u>, as to the Lord, and not unto men...

No, I'm not a coach or a professional – I'm simply a fellow who took up golf upon retirement. These gleanings are a result of my research into how to play the necessary shots and the strategies needed to improve my game. However, someone once said that the game of golf is too hard a game to try to play like someone else. **So, when trying out these tips, remember that you may need to make your own personal adjustments.**

Furthermore, don't get too downhearted when things go wrong. It is often said, among even the best of golfers, that the only thing consistent about golf is its inconsistency. Nevertheless, I hope these gleanings will be helpful to you.

Please note, some of the instruction was gained (over the years) during lessons from different coaches, for which I was grateful. Further instruction was gained from a spread of tips by coaches and players on the internet or in books.

The cartoons and "Spot the Golfer" pictures are included to lighten what can be an intense subject.

Basic.

The diagram below shows a simplified position of feet relative to the ball position for various clubs. Note: the ball is in the forward position when the driver is used. The driver has the longest shaft of all the clubs; therefore, the ball is shown to be further away from the feet but square to the left heel (for the right-hander). The toe of the front foot is angled forwards a little to make turning easier.

In general, the wedges have the shortest shafts, therefore the ball is shown to be closer to the feet and back (slightly) towards the right foot. However, the feet may be drawn closer together when playing these short irons. The long irons will maintain a wider stance. The medium irons will have a narrower stance.

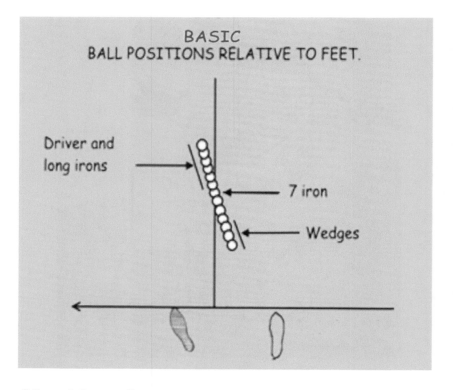

More Advanced.

The ball positions in the picture below are based on advice found in the book "Ben Hogan's Five Lessons – The Modern Fundamentals of Golf". This differs from the first diagram, in that the ball's position remains square to the target line and only the distance on that line changes. In other words, the ball is brought closer to the feet for the medium and short irons. Furthermore, only the rear foot changes its position being brought closer to the one on the left and, at the same time, moving it forwards slightly towards the ball. Note that the toes

6

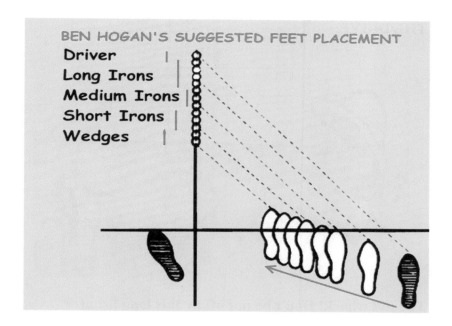

of the feet are aligned from in to out (called "a closed stance") for the longer clubs; but they are in a more out-to-in for the shortest clubs (called "an open stance).

THE DRIVE.

The full whack! Don't be put off by this long list of instructions!

- Tee the ball high (half the ball showing above the club height). The material of the tee itself makes no real difference to the drive as the ball is compressed quickly and moving away before the club hits it. If you look at the slow-motion videos of the moment of impact on the Internet, you will see this.
- Stand parallel to the target line with your feet together. The ball should be in front of you in line with the slit between your feet.

- Move leading foot (left) 5-10cms towards the target.
- Move the trailing foot backwards so the final width of the stance is the width of your shoulders. Too wide and your turn will be hampered.

8

- Bend the knees slightly.
- Bend forward from the hips keeping a relatively straight back.
- Grip the club with a light firmness (about 4 out of 10 with 10 being the hardest grip you can make). There should be about 2-4cms free at the top of the shaft.

(If you tend to slice (ball flight bends right), use what is called a "strong" grip in the sense that the left hand is turned to the right a little to reveal at least three knuckles of the left hand. In the normal grip two to three knuckles are visible. The pictures below show the strength of grips and the Vardon Grip).

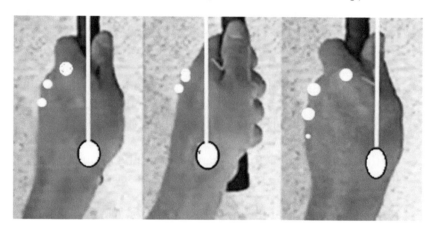

| Normal | Weak | Strong |

- Allow the club to hover about 12cms behind the ball at address.
- Then lean to the right a little (head is behind the ball). The left arm is kept straight (though relaxed) through the take-away in the backswing.
- Weight is equal on both feet and towards the balls of the feet.
- Relax the torso so it may turn easily.

- Focus eyes on a point of strike on the ball.
- Draw the club back steadily parallel to the ground at the start.
- Turn your back to the target during the backswing (Note: the left shoulder dips to come under the chin).
- Hinge the wrists as you approach the top of the swing.
- Behind your head the club should reach a point parallel to the ground and pointing to the target for a full swing; but a three-quarter swing gives more control.
- The weight is shifted (60-70%) to the right at this point.
- Start turning the hips towards the target at the start of the downswing.
- The first movement of the arms is to drop almost vertically maintaining the wrist hinge.
- Swing towards the ball (holding the hinged wrist) position until the hands are about thigh height.
- Keep wrists quite relaxed and don't try to force (smash) the ball forwards – let the club and swing do the job.
- Extend your right arm – as if throwing a stone to skim on water.
- At the point of impact your hands should be about 10cms on the target side of the ball and your wrists should be unhinging.
- Remember to swing through the ball – not at it.
- Extend through.
- Complete the follow-through to finish facing the target and the club well over the left shoulder.

Note.

This is far too much to remember when first approaching the golf drive. So, using the normal grip, try the following to develop the swing more naturally.

- Start swinging back and forth without a ball ensuring you turn your torso left and right fully without exerting speed. If it helps, lift (a little) the right and left heels consecutively as you do so.

- Then increase the speed of the swing until you hear the club swish *after* the swing has bottomed out.
- Next, do short swings with a ball in the way without forcing speed. Slowly increase the length of the swing and the speed noting your change in distance.
- When striking consistently, work on fine-tuning the ball's direction by opening or closing the club's face a little at a time.

Drills To Increase Swing Speed.

Drill 1:

- Grip your driver up at the head end and hold the shaft horizontally out in front of you. Swing the club around you, keeping the shaft horizontal. Try to create the loudest swish you can achieve. This will come when you allow your lower body rotation to pull the club forward, your hands and arms arriving later.
- Flip the club the right way round and repeat.
- Finally, do the same slowly lowering the swing until in the normal swing position.

Drill 2:

- Set up for your swing.
- Pull your left foot back close to right one.
- As you start the downswing, step forward with left foot as though stamping a tee into the ground with it and complete the swing. This encourages power in the weight shift.

Drill 3:

- Do a wide arc in your backswing hinging your wrists slightly at shoulder height.
- Start the downswing hinging the wrists more and holding the angle as you come down.
- Start unhinging about hip height.
- Snap the club forward and through with the swish after the ball.
- Release and complete the swing.

Advanced – The Draw and Fade.

Here we will consider how to draw and fade a ball.

The Draw.

A draw involves the ball starting to the right of the target line then curving left to finish on target. It is a shot for driver, long woods and long irons. Some coaches would say short irons as well, but there is more of a tendency to hook these. Here is a *basic* way to achieve the draw:

A DRAW

1. Aim your feet, hips and shoulders *slightly* to the right of the target. (This should automatically develop an 'in-to-out' swing path as you swing along the line of your feet).
2. Move your grip slightly clockwise so you can see an extra knuckle on your left hand (a stronger grip).

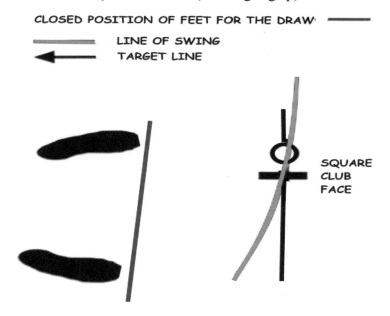

CLOSED POSITION OF FEET FOR THE DRAW ▬▬

▬▬▬ LINE OF SWING

◀▬▬ TARGET LINE

SQUARE
CLUB
FACE

3. Set the ball level with the heel of your leading foot.
4. Set and keep your clubface square to the ball and the target.
5. Strike the ball feeling like you are following through right of the target.
6. Complete with a full extension and follow-through.

This golfer has a natural draw which, at times results in hooks. Who is he?

SPOT THE GOLFER.

The Fade.

A FADE

A fade relates to a shot where the ball starts left and moves right through the air. Here is a basic way to achieve the fade:

1. Aim your feet and shoulders to the left of the target. (This should automatically develop an 'out-to-in' swing path as you swing along the line of your feet).

15

2. Grip the club normally, but a little more tightly with the three fingers of your left hand.
3. Set the ball level with the heel of your leading foot.
4. Set your clubface square to the ball and the target.
5. Strike the ball feeling as though you are following through left of the target.
6. Complete full follow through.

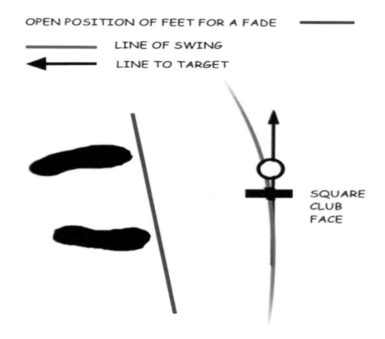

OPEN POSITION OF FEET FOR A FADE ━━━

━━━━━━━ LINE OF SWING

◀━━━━━━ LINE TO TARGET

SQUARE CLUB FACE

Butch Harmon taught this golfer how to fade the ball. Who is he?

Adjusting to a tailwind.

With a following wind, use the three wood instead of the driver. This gives more height and less spin making for a straight shot which is blown along.

Adjusting to a headwind.

When playing into the wind hit the driver more softly. A headwind exaggerates any spin on the ball, so slices and hooks will result if you drive hard.

Alternatively, punch the ball into the wind using a 3 or 4 iron.

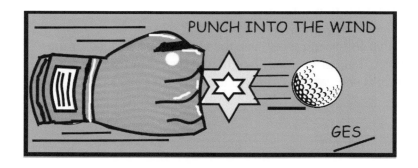

PUNCH INTO THE WIND

GES

HIT THE HOLE!

O	F	O	U	R	S	O	M	E	S	O	G	S	S
C	D	S	Y	G	I	B	U	N	K	E	R	O	C
R	D	R	A	C	E	R	O	C	S	F	L	A	G
V	V	E	Y	C	I	A	R	E	P	I	E	P	E
B	H	Y	B	R	I	D	D	F	M	A	V	E	R
M	M	H	R	E	R	A	B	P	A	D	R	O	H
I	T	O	V	I	D	R	A	Y	I	P	S	A	D
I	G	I	T	F	R	E	D	H	D	O	Z	S	D
I	F	E	F	E	A	C	C	R	T	A	D	W	S
F	S	A	C	E	E	D	D	I	R	O	N	R	R
F	T	E	F	D	R	O	E	D	U	D	O	R	U
C	W	O	O	D	B	D	R	A	W	E	D	K	A
A	D	D	W	H	D	P	U	T	T	E	R	N	O
D	E	O	R	L	R	R	E	V	I	R	D	D	Y

IRON
SCORECARD
TEE
HAZARD
BUNKER
DRIVER
DRAW
FLAG
PUTTER
YIPS
DIVOT
FOURSOMES
FADE
HYBRID
WOOD

USING THE THREE WOOD.

In general, the three wood is a difficult club to use when in a fairway lie; but can be a powerful tool for the golfer once mastered. It has a loft of 13-16 degrees, so golfers often think they must manoeuvre the ball into the air. This is not necessary. When swung correctly, the distance and height take care of themselves.

From The Fairway.

- Place ball a little forward (left) of the centre of your stance.
- The centre of your body should line up with the clubhead at address.
- Use a slightly downward strike taking a very thin divot (or scuffing the surface of the ground) in front of the ball.
- At least a three-quarters backswing is required. With weight transferring more to the back leg. (Trying to hit a three wood softer is very difficult).
- The downswing begins with the hips moving forward.
- It should be fluent and a little in to out.

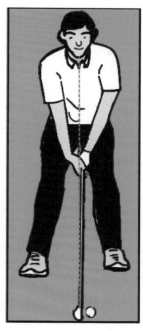

- Try to meet the ball with the clubface square to the target.
- Follow through – all the way! This ensures the "release" of the club.

If you find the ball swings right, then use a "stronger" grip.

Do not try to "hammer" the ball. Your arms will tighten and raise the club. You will likely "top" the ball.

From The Tee.

- The stance is like that used for the driver.
- The ball is teed up so a third to a half of the ball is above the club face's crown.
- The swing imitates that used for the driver.

A Drill For Practising The Sweeping Action Of The Three Wood.

- Use two ball-size pieces of card. Place one where the ball would be and the other 15cm in front of it.
- Set up to the "card ball" and on the downswing train yourself to hit both pieces of card. This is ensuring an extension in the swing.

We shall play our golf, whatever the cost may be. We shall play from the roots, the long grass and gorse. We shall play from the puddles, the sands and the banks. We shall play from the ditches, the tracks and the slopes. We shall never surrender.

THE SEVEN-IRON SHOT.

The average leisure golfer may hit a 7-iron between 120 -160 yards. These instructions, therefore, give a basis for the swing for the mid-iron shots (irons 6, 7 and 8) with only the ball position varying very slightly forward for the lower *number* (6) and back for the higher (8).

Steps.

- Stand with feet and shoulders in line with ball slightly front of centre of stance.
- Club face square to target.
- With club face in position behind the ball grip with the left hand so that the handle lies between the top bend of the forefinger and the base of the little finger. You can check this by holding your left arm straight out and holding the club in your fingers only so that it points vertically skywards – forming a right angle between club and arm. You can then add your thumb and then the right hand to the grip.
- The thumb should be almost on top of the handle of the shaft pointing towards the ball (you should be able to see two finger knuckles as you look down).
- Fold your right hand over the bottom of the left so that the left thumb lies under the heel of the right thumb and the right little finger sits on the line of the gap between the weak and little fingers of the left hand (see "Vardon Grip" picture).
- The back of the thumb of the right hand should point to the right shoulder.
- Feet - shoulder width apart.
- Right foot square to target. Left foot angled slightly forward.
- Torso leans forward from the waist (back straight).
- Legs slightly bent.
- There should then be about an open hand's span between the body and the top of the club's handle.

21

- Weight of the body towards the balls of the feet and more on right foot.
- At this point the right shoulder drops naturally below the left.
- The backswing begins with a turning of the hips away from the target. Hips, shoulders/arms and hands are activated in that order.
- The left arm remains straight for as long as comfortably possible in the backswing (arms should, however, be quite relaxed).
- The right arm bends at the elbow pointing downwards.
- The club rises to a point above your head where it is parallel to the ground.
- Begin the downswing by shifting your weight onto your left foot. This is vital as it moves the low point of your swing slightly forwards of the ball enabling you to take a divot. During the swing do not try to force the ball by pushing with the right hand. Allow the speed of rotation and the club to do the work recognising that you come down at the back of the ball rather than trying to scoop it up. A divot should be taken.
- At impact the shoulders should be in line with the target, the hands should be in front of the ball and the grip should be firm (see drawing right).
- Continue the swing until the body is facing the target. Note that the left foot remains still and weight finishes on it.
- The right foot moves to show the shoe's sole at impact to accommodate the follow through. The movement completes up on the toe with the sole seen behind.

Spot the Golfer.

GES

Drills to get the feeling of the weight shifts in a swing.

1. At set up, place a straight cane parallel to the target line and place the balls of your feet on it when taking your stance. The weight at the start is evenly spread. In the backswing shift your weight to the heel of your back foot. On the downswing shift your weight to the ball of your right foot. (You can take this further by playing the shot; but follow the weight through by walking after the ball).

2. Practise swings with your back foot standing on an object which is about 10cms high. This encourages you to shift your weight forwards on the downswing.

3. Set up normally and make your backswing. As it approaches the top, lift your left foot a little from the ground and replace it firmly as you start the downswing to take your weight. The back foot will make its normal movement to show the shoe sole (right up on the toe).

4. Take your normal stance and mark your feet positions using two tees. Then draw your front foot back to the rear foot. Make your back-lift. As you reach the top move the front foot back to its original position. Swing down and through as you do so.

Drills to help you come down on the ball.

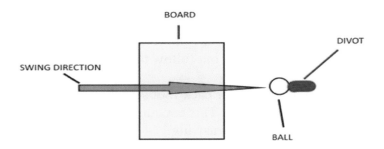

1. Take a piece of board (ply or laminated hardboard about A4 size). Place it about 15cms behind your ball. Take your shot. If the club hits the board, you are not coming down on the ball enough. Adjust your swing and weight until you're missing the

board and striking the ball crisply. You should be producing a shallow divot just after the ball position.

2a. Take your stance to a ball and then move the ball so its sits in front of your back ankle rather than in the middle of the stance. Swing to an imaginary ball in the middle without hitting the ball at the ankle position.

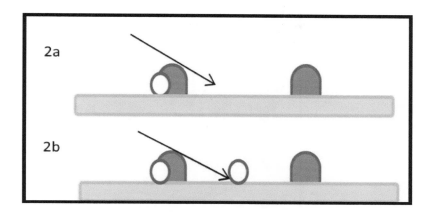

2b. When you have done that successfully a number of times, keep the back ankle ball where it is and place a ball in the middle of the stance; but this time set your club up to the back ball – do your backswing but then come down to hit the front ball keeping your hands forward at impact.

Drills for speeding up the downswing.

1. Take your stance so that your feet and knees are together. Starting with a half-swing strike the ball forwards keeping the feet together and maintaining balance. Try again making a longer swing. Built it up until swinging as fully as possible.
2. Try the same again with a towel stretched from under your armpits and across your chest. Don't drop the towel as you swing.

THE LOB SHOT.

The lob shot carries high over relatively short distances and the ball stops quickly on landing.

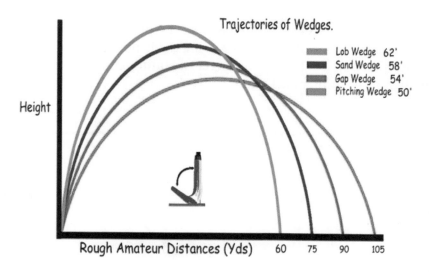

Trajectories of Wedges.

▬	Lob Wedge	62'
▬	Sand Wedge	58'
▬	Gap Wedge	54'
▬	Pitching Wedge	50'

Height

Rough Amateur Distances (Yds)   60   75   90   105

- Use a sand wedge or lob wedge.
- Feet - shoulder width apart.
- Aim your feet left of the hole in the stance (open).
- Weight is more left.
- Place the ball a little in front of the middle of stance.
- Open the clubface a little (but it should be aiming square to the target).
- Re-grip.
- Top of club handle should point towards your belly button.
- Assess amount of backswing required for the distance of travel.
- Rotate body during backswing (the body moving the arms initially).
- Swing club forward in line with the feet keeping club face open.

27

- Hands are slightly in front of the ball at strike.

Follow through as comfortable for the distance. (This can only be determined through practise).

Note:
Additional distance can be found either by putting the ball further back in the stance or by having the hands a little more forward at impact. There is a danger of cutting into the ground with the ball further back though.

THE PITCH-SHOT.

In a pitch-shot, the ball carries through the air a good distance (at least 10 yards) and stops quickly on landing.

- Feet – almost shoulder width apart and slightly open to target.
- Ball in middle of stance.
- Grip with thumbs down the front of handle.
- Start backswing by turning the body (the body moves the arms initially).
- Hinge left wrist a little earlier on backswing.
- Use no more than three-quarters of your normal backswing adjusting the length of its arc according to the distance to be carried.
- Swing so hands are slightly in front of the ball at strike.
- Aim for a ball then turf contact.
- Follow through so chest faces the target.

There are three techniques for pitching that you may like to try. They are:

1. The Triangular: this complies with the advice given in the above but emphasizes that the triangle formed by the shoulders and arms is maintained and the wrists are not hinged

2. The Hinge and Hold: again, the basics are the same, but the wrists are hinged early. The hands are in front of the club face at impact and the follow through is towards the flag and held. This may be implemented from waist to waist or shoulder to shoulder depending on the distance.

3. The Linear: the stance is similar, but at impact the club shaft is vertical towards the sternum. The swing is like that for the triangular, but there is some wrist hinge.

THE CHIP-SHOT

In a chip-shot, the ball carries a little and rolls a lot.

Test out this principle for yourselves when chipping. On a level surface, in normal conditions and using a putting stroke, the "Rule of 12" comes into force. That is to say, if you carry the ball a certain distance then the roll will be proportional. See the diagram and table below. So, the **8** iron will cause the ball to roll **4** times the carry distance: 8 + 4 = 12. Adjustments may be made to this depending on your personal stroke and the firmness of the green and the slope of the green. However, this rule only applies if the ball is less than 10 yards from the green. If the ball is **pitched** (rather than chipped) over 12 yards or more, it does not apply as the height in the carry reduces the rolling distance too much. In the **chip-shot** the following apply:

- Legs only slightly apart.
- Use an open stance (aiming feet left of target).
- Place ball back a little in the stance (for more roll), or

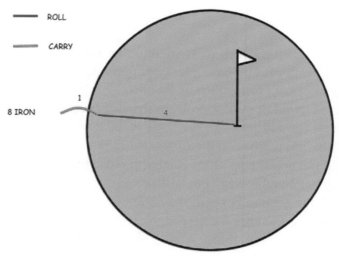

CHIPPING RATIO OF CARRY AND ROLL USING A PUTTING STROKE

31

- Place the ball forward in your stance (for more height).
- Weight on leading foot.
- Grip the club about 5cms further down handle than usual. (The grip should be as for a full swing).
- Keep hands forward of the ball.
- Bend knees a little more than usual.
- Aim the club's face square to the target.
- Choose the spot you want the ball to land. Note: if you

Carry/Roll	Level	Up slope	Down slope
1:2	Pitching wedge	9 iron	Sand wedge
1:3	9 iron	8 iron	Pitching wedge
1:4	8 iron	7 iron	9 iron
1:5	7 iron	6 iron	8 iron
1:6	6 iron	5 iron	7 iron

have little green to work with, hit a higher shot that hits and rolls very little. If you have plenty of green to work with, hit a lower shot so it rolls more like a putt.
- Use the pendulum motion from the shoulders for the shot as you do for putting.
- Backswing relative to the distance to the target spot.
- Keep the upper part of the lead arm close to chest.
- Keep head and lower body still.
- Brush the ground beneath the ball.
- Accelerate the club face through impact with hands in front of the ball; follow through and hold. The chest should be facing the target.

34, North Hill Rd.,
Ipswich,
IP4 2PN.

Dear Chris,

Please find the free books - including "Golf Gleanings". Use them as you will.

Sincerely,

George.

It may prove useful to set up and then take a deep breath. As you start the backswing start releasing the breath steadily and do so throughout the swing. Apparently, this keeps the muscles relaxed.

If chipping from clover or deeper lies, it will help to use a nine iron with a closed face and punch the ball more.

Phil Nicholson chips in a different way. He hinges his wrists on the short back swing and keeps his hands in front of the ball at impact. His follow through is short and to a holding position. Hence, the chip is by the "hinge and hold method". I have to confess that I find the impact on the ball is purer using this method but controlling the distance is more difficult.

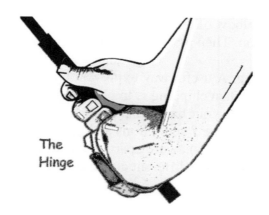

The Hinge

Drills to help chipping.

1. For loft, balance a club horizontally on the top of a brick (or some other object) and place your ball 2 yards behind the middle of it. Chip the ball over the club. Remember, it is a descending blow. When you have succeeded a few times, move the ball a closer and repeat the process. Alternatively,

you could add another brick and strike from a variety of distances.

2. (For distance). Place a hoop (or door mat) about 3 yards from you and try chipping so that the ball lands in it. After 3 consecutive successful chips, move back a half-yard and repeat until successful. Move further back and repeat the process. (If landing on a green note the distance of roll onwards).

3. (For different lofts). Using the left hand only, your weight forward and the ball back in your stance strike a few balls and observe what happens. The flight of the ball should be low. Then repeat the shot using your right hand only, your club open and the ball in the middle of your stance. The flight should be higher.

4. How to keep the back arm relatively straight: cut out a piece of cardboard from a stiff box about 14 x 8 inches. Wrap it round the elbow of the back arm using elastic bands to hold it in position. Then practise chipping using one of the drills above.

5. Stop flicking. A useful way to prevent trying to flick the ball into the air when chipping is to play your shot as usual but at impact remove your back hand from the club.

6. Chipping with the 7 and 9 irons and the sand wedge. Place two canes (or clubs) a yard apart and some distance from you. Then using the different clubs, chip to land between the

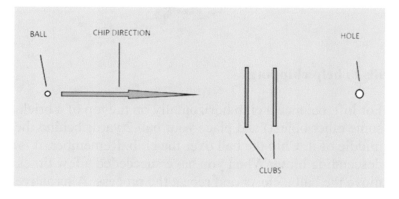

canes paying special attention to how far the golf ball rolls on. (See picture above).

7. Using different clubs but the same power of stroke, chip the ball and note the differences in roll on a flat green.

CREATING BACKSPIN USING A WEDGE.

Conditions:

- Backspin will not bite much if the ground is hard.
- To create backspin effectively requires a good lie with no grass between the club and the ball.
- A good quality ball is needed preferably with a softer covering that encourages spin (e.g., Titleist Pro V1 or Niki 20xis or Srixon Z-Star).
- The spin will bite in softer conditions or where there is a backward slope on the green.
- Spin is more effective if there is a headwind.
- In the main, backspin is used to slow down the ball quickly rather than reversing it. It lands "softly".

Steps:

Use a sand wedge or pitching wedge.

- Make sure your club is clean so that the mill and grooves are effective in imparting spin. Set your body slightly open to your target. This means you aim your feet and shoulders left of the target (if righthanded) depending on the distance to cover. The more the distance, the greater the angle of stance.
- Lean your weight (60-70%) towards your front leg.
- Play the ball in the centre of your stance to begin with. (Later, try with it slightly back or forward to see which has the best results for you).
- At address, your hands should be a little in front of the ball.
- Open the wedge a little and re-grip.
- The backswing should be straight back initially.
- Hinge your wrists early.
- Judge the length of the backswing according to the distance to the target.
- Swing normally.

- Make sure you strike the ball near its base before skimming the ground. Only a short, shallow divot (if any) should appear in front of the initial ball position.
- Your hands should be just in front of the ball as you strike the ball.
- Remember to follow through.

TAKING A DIVOT.

If the ball is sitting on the ground and you are using an iron, you should always take a shallow divot to ensure that you get a full-face impact on the ball. The bounce (the angle of the sole of the club) is there to stop the club digging into the ground too much. To ensure a divot you must hit the ball a split second before hitting the ground. Therefore, the divot will start a little forward of the base of the golf ball and will be shallow (a bacon slice) and roughly 8–12cms long.

To achieve this, your hands should be a little forward of the ball at impact and your weight forward on your left leg.

38

39

PLAYING A BUNKER SHOT.

From dry sand.

Conditions.
- About 10-12 yards to target.
- Sand dry.
- Level position.

Steps:

- Set your stance open aiming about 3-4 yards left of the target. Work your feet well into the sand to get a firm base.
- The ball should be between middle and front foot of stance.
- Open the sand wedge but square to the target.

- Set up to hit the sand about 5-10cms behind the ball (do not touch the sand when preparing).
- The handle of the club should point towards your belly button.
- Break your wrists early in the backswing.
- Keep your head still.
- Take the swing back to just pass your head.
- Swing down into and through the sand (lifting about a 4mm thickness of sand). You must commit to the shot.
- Hands should be forward of ball at impact.
- Follow through completely.

From wet sand.

Conditions:

- About 10-12 yards to target.
- Sand wet
- Ball possibly plugged.
- Level position.

Steps:

- Set your stance aiming square to the target.
- Work your feet well into the sand to get a firm base.
- The ball should be between middle and front of stance.
- Use the lob wedge.
- Have the wedge square to the target.
- Set up to hit the sand about 5-10 cms behind the ball (do not touch the sand when preparing). If plugged, then hit the sand further away from the ball to get under it.
- Use a wide arc in your backswing.
- Keep your head still.

- Take the swing back to the vertical position with wrists hinged.

- Keep your hands forward of place of impact.
- Swing into and through the sand.
- Follow through fully, if possible.

Playing from steep-sided bunker.

Conditions:

- About 10-12 yards to target.
- Sand dry.
- Bunker sides steep and deep.
- Level position.

Steps:

- Set your stance aiming about 3-4 yards left of the target.
- The ball should be between middle and front foot of stance.
- Open the sand wedge.
- Set up to hit the sand about 5-10cms behind the ball (do not touch the sand when preparing).
- Use a wider arc in your backswing.
- Keep your head still.
- Take the shaft back to just past your head with wrists hinged.
- Swing into and through the sand (lifting about a double wafer thickness of sand).
- Follow through.

Notes.

In the case of the ball lying on an uphill slope your weight should be more on the back foot *with your shoulders parallel to the slope. The ball should be forward in the stance.
*Some coaches advise an even weight distribution.

If on a downhill slope, have your weight more on the front foot with the ball in the middle or slightly back in the stance. Your shoulders should parallel the slope. Also be sensible. If the lie of the ball is in a very difficult position in the bunker, consider playing in the direction of the easiest exit.

SHOTS FROM IRREGULAR LIES.

From divots.

Avoid using a club with a high bounce factor like a sand-wedge because you are going to make another divot as you play the shot. Choose an iron relative to distance needed. More weight on the left foot. Use a three-quarter swing and come down on the ball keeping hands forward.

Uphill Shots.

This is a normal swing with clubs chosen for the distance. However, the ball will tend to fly a little left, so allow for this. Also, place the ball further forward in your stance and ensure your shoulders are parallel to the slope on which you are standing.

Downhill shots.

This is a normal swing with clubs chosen for the distance. However, the ball will tend to fly a little right, so allow for this. Also, place the ball further back in your stance and ensure your shoulders are parallel to the slope on which you are standing.

With ball above feet on side slope.

The ball will tend to go left so allow for this by aiming right of your target. Grip down on your club to shorten it a bit. Weight is on the balls of your feet. Knees are not bent so much as normal. Take a practice shot to ensure it is the right length. Use a three-quarter swing. Otherwise, the swing is normal.

With ball below feet on side slope.

The ball will tend to go right so allow for this by aiming left of your target. Grip high on the grip of the club. Bend your knees more than usual with weight on heels. Take a practise shot to ensure the club is the right length. Use a three-quarter swing. Otherwise, the swing is normal.

From light rough.

Use wedges and medium irons unless the back of the ball is clearly seen so longer clubs may be used. Grip club more tightly with last three fingers of the left hand (for right-handers). Have the ball in the middle of the stance. Hinge early in the backswing and come down on the ball. If the ball is sitting up, then sweep the ball away instead of coming down. Note: if the grass is growing towards you, the stroke will be more difficult. If away from you it will be easier.

From heavy rough.

This is like a bunker shot. Use a slightly open sand or pitching wedge to bring the ball into play on the closest part of the fairway. Stand with ball in back third of stance. Grip firmly.

Hinge wrists early. Come down on the back of the ball (from out-to-in) and limit your follow through to prevent a double hit.

Hard ground.

Use a three-quarter swing with a club relative to achieve the distance required. Ball in the middle of the stance. Sweep the ball away but be aware that the ball will have more backspin than usual. Remember, hands in front of the ball at impact and follow through.

From loose lies.

The shot will depend on the depth at which the ball lies. Choose your irons accordingly. Clear the loose impediments in the direction your swing comes into the ball and at the front where the ball will travel. The ball must not move when you do

this. The swing is fairly normal for a high-sitting ball and like a bunker shot for a ball sitting low.

PUTTING.

Games are won and lost on the putting green. It is a vital part of your game.

The first thing to do is make sure the putter is the right length. The easiest way to do this is to assume a regular putting stance, with your arms hanging down. The length of the putter should come up from the ground to the top of one of your hands. As the normal  putter is 34 inches long then you could mark your top-of-the-hand position using some tape on the handle. This will then ensure that your arms are not bent too much nor too straight when making the stroke.

Find your dominant eye. Make a circular window with the index fingers and thumbs of your hands with your arms stretched forwards. Look through the window at an object with two eyes open. Close one eye. If the object stays in the window without jumping across that is the dominant eye. Use this eye when lining up the golf ball for a putt.

The next thing to realize is that putts of professionals from 3 feet have a 97-100% chance of success. From 4 feet a 90% chance. From 5 feet a 75%. Finally, from 6 feet a 55%. So, try to get chips and long putts into that three feet range for putting success.

Also recognize three times as many downhill putts are missed relative to uphill ones.

You may mark your ball's position on the green (with a small coin or plastic marker or similar object) in order to lift it to clean, or to line it up. Make sure you put the marker down before lifting the ball or it is a one stroke penalty. Replace the ball when ready before taking away the marker.

Have a thin, straight line of about 5cm length drawn on your ball with an indelible pen.

With your dominant eye, line this marked line up with the track that you want the ball to follow in order to hole out. Ensure the line is right on top of the placed ball. (If there's no line on the ball, you may find some kind of mark on the green close to you that is in line with the track you wish to follow. You can aim for that).

Alternatively, if you have a line on the head of the putter, place your eyes over it and line it up with the line of the ball. Then trust your set up and relax to play the shot. I, personally, find it useful to gaze at the hole for two or three seconds before making the stroke. This gives a fix on distance. Then, look at the ball until the stroke has been made.

Any loose impediments along the line of the putt may be removed (but no pressing down is allowed at this time of writing).

Use the putter on the green, although you can use the other clubs if you wish. Look at local rules to see if this is allowed.

Stand with feet and shoulders in line with the target. Feet should be far enough apart for firm balance.

Your weight should be more towards the balls of your feet.

Lean forwards so the eyes are over or almost over the ball to set the aim, set the club position and then move your head towards your body a little and slightly behind the ball. Mind you don't change the club-head position as you do so.

The ball should be slightly forward in the stance so that you strike the ball just after the putter has starting its upswing. This puts top spin on the ball and helps it to stay on a straight course.

Ensure that the arc made by the putter swing is a shallow one. It is more difficult to control a straight back and straight forward method but ensure the follow-through is toward the target.

Grips vary and may be complicated, but I simply follow the grip described for the 7-iron described previously, but extend the forefinger of my right hand down the shaft so it's top joint bends just below the handle.

Three grips may be seen above. From left to right: the conventional grip, the cross-over grip and the claw grip. Use one that is comfortable for you. Do not grip too tightly.

The length of the backswing should correspond to the distance the ball has to travel. This is discovered by practising.

The forward swing goes through the ball some distance before stopping. The follow through is toward the hole all the time.

The swing is produced from the movement of the shoulders (swing the club like a pendulum), rather than pushing with the hands and arms. The arms remain quiet and the wrists remain set throughout. The rest of the body and the head remain still.

I, personally, aim to reach just beyond the back of the cup (20cms) if the green is flat. (Some coaches recommend about 40cms past to avoid borrows immediately around the hole).

An uphill putt will require a strike to go further past the cup. A steeper downward slope may mean aiming for a spot between you and the cup. Remember, a putt that's short has no chance at all of going in. When quite close to a hole on a steep slope, use the toe end of your putter's face.

It is always best to "miss" on the top side of a hole on a slope. It has a greater chance of dropping in.

Also, you can hit the ball more firmly if the putt is uphill because the back of the cup is higher and the ball, bumping into it, is more likely to drop in.

To bear in mind.

- If the green has been mown, then you may have light and dark lines on it. These are produced by the way the grass is lying (as on a garden lawn). If the blades of grass (dark) are pointing towards you the ball will slow faster. If pointing away (light), the ball will run further.

- If the green is wet, the ball slows down much more quickly.
- If dry, it runs further.
- Be aware of the direction of any strong wind and adjust your line or length of backswing (if with or against you) accordingly.
- Note whether the green is going uphill or downhill and allow for it.
- Read the green so that you understand its various undulations and allow for them.
- To read the green you need to assess its slope as you approach it comparing it with the local surroundings.
- From the side of your putting line, see if the green is sloping up or down from your ball to the hole.
- From behind your ball, see if the green has any slopes going across the line of your putt.
- Especially note any undulations at the hole itself as a slow-moving ball will respond to these more. This is a reason why, as mentioned previously, with some shortish putts, professionals may strike the ball quite firmly.
- One old-fashioned way of determining a general borrow is to squat behind your ball and suspend your putter in front of you to act as a plumb line. (You should know this position by having tested the putter against a vertical object like a door post). If the ball and hole are covered then there is no borrow. But if you see more of the hole to one side of the putter then adjust your putting line accordingly. This may also be done from behind the hole looking back through it towards the ball. So, if your feet are on a slight slope, your plumbline will indicate it. Be warned, this is not the most reliable of methods especially if there are other rises and falls between you and the hole.
- Note also, that if there is a slight cross slope near your ball on a *longish* putt, then the slope may have no effect on the

ball in the first yard or more because the speed of the ball annuls the borrow.

Note: I personally use my fingers (digits) to assess a slope running across my line of putt. I stand with my arm outstretched with my hand over the ball. I raise one finger to ascertain the target for a slight slope. A severe slope would be the distance covered by five digits. The 2, 3 and 4 fingers likewise for slopes in between the extremes. (See the diagram below).

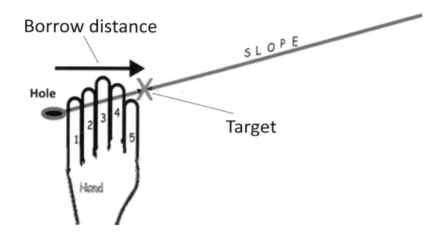

Lie Angle.

The putter has a lie angle. It should be such that the eyes are over the ball when the sole of the putter is flat on the ground.

Swing-weight.

Swing-weight of a putter varies from light to heavy. See which best fits your stroke. Many golfers prefer a putter with a heavier swing-weight to encourage a smooth, rhythmic motion.

Judging distances longer than 6 yards.

1. Do you underestimate distance? Test yourself.
2. Stand by your ball and look at the hole (black dots).
3. Close your eyes and point to where you think the hole is (red circle).
4. Open your eyes and note the spot to which you are pointing (red).
5. If it falls short of the hole add that distance (blue line) to your putt beyond the hole (X).

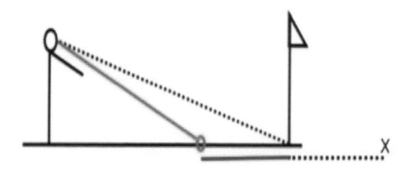

(NB The diagram is exaggerated).

Judging distance from the side may be more productive. This gives you much better assessment of the putt length.

Measure the putt length by pacing it out. Then rehearse the putt before making it. Some research has found that using your eyes and hands in tandem enhances brain perception.
Read the green of an *uphill putt* from behind the ball.
Read the green of a *downhill putt* from below the hole.

Reading putts from a clock-face.

When you reach the green, picture a clock on top of the hole in front of you. As you assess the line, imagine where on the clock your putt will roll over and fall into the cup. Then, simply react to that position on the clock face.

Pitch marks.

Repair of pitch marks on the green is important. Don't lever the dent upwards. This breaks the grass roots and leaves air pockets beneath. Always push **in** vertically at the sides and lever the ground inwards towards the centre of the dent. When repaired, then use the sole of the putter to flatten it.

Uphill and downhill putts.

On a slight slope upward, aim 20 cms past the hole. As the slope steepens make that distance longer accordingly. On steep slopes remember the uphill hole will look shorter than it actually is.

The downhill hole will look further away than it is. So hit to a point before the hole adjusting accordingly as the slope becomes steeper.

Putting Practise Drills.

Drill 1.
Place balls in concentric circles around a hole. Try putting the inside balls first in sequence then move to the next etc. Balls may be added in wider "circles" as proficiency increases (see diagram below).

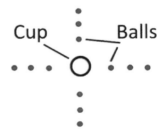

Drill 2.
Another game is to practise "Putting Bowls" with a partner to see who can finish nearer the coloured ball used for a jack.

56

Drill 3.
Try longer putts to a line or the fringe of a green.

Drill 4.
Putt to a tee increasing the distance as you improve.

Drill 5.
For longer putts put a semi-circle of tees at 40cm from the back of the hole. Putt to the hole. If the ball doesn't reach, that's a one-point penalty. If it goes into the tee semi-circle, that's one point to you. If it goes in the hole, that's two points to you. Play with a partner or two. Change distances with improvement.

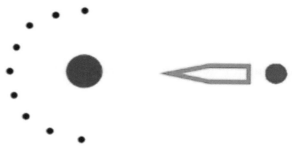

Drill 6.
Improve your back and forward stroke by setting up, then, only looking at the hole, play the stroke. Remember to follow through towards the hole.

Drill 7.
Make a parallel gate for your putting stroke using clubs, sticks or tees to ensure a straight back straight forward stroke. See diagram below.

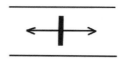

Drill 8.
After doing drill 6 set up and make the stroke looking at the
ball only.

Drill 9.

There are various videos on You Tube that suggest a method to
gain a rhythmic swing in putting using a metronome. I would
suggest the number of beats at about 80 beats per minute. Set
two large coins (C1 and C2 on the diagram) 20cms apart with a
small coin at the midpoint. Match the swing of the putter to the
metronome's arm movement swinging from coin to coin. Once
a comfortable rhythm has been established, move the front and
rear coins further apart e.g., 30cms. You will now have to
swing a little faster to keep time. Once mastered extend the
distance further and repeat the process. Then go to the green
with the metronome and do the same but with a ball at the
midpoint. Measure the length the ball travels for the different
swing lengths.

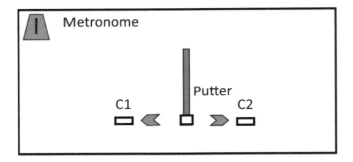

The bump and run with the putter.

The "bump and run" with a putter is a shot played near the
green which flies little and runs a lot. It is used in dry
conditions when a short chip or pitch would be more difficult to
stop on the green. The putter does have a little loft so playing
the ball in the middle of the stance will encourage the ball to

lift a little initially and then run on. Keep the hands forward when playing it.

A further development of this (when within a yard of the green) is to come down onto the ball hitting it groundward. It bounces over the thicker grass to run on when it finds the green.

A FIVE-MINUTE WARM UP.

Pre-round five-minute warm-up

The warm-up is very important for injury prevention. You need to get the blood flowing through your body so that you warm your muscles up, and that involves increasing your heart rate a bit.

1. Jog on the spot for a minute or two.
2. Make gentle windmill movements with your arms straight both forwards and backwards.
3. Several lunges like a fencer with a slow stretch, rather than jerking.
4. Then move into the exercises listed under "At the Driving Range".

AT THE DRIVING RANGE.

Preliminary warm up.

- Place a club behind your shoulder blades and make gentle 90-degree rotations to the left and to the right.
- Make similar turns with the club across your chest while standing in the normal address position.
- Hold a club out horizontal to the ground. Swing it back and forth - slowly getting lower until you're sweeping the mat.
- Make some swishes with the left hand only and then the other way with the right hand only. You'll probably find you have more club speed with the right hand if right-handed. A pity isn't it. Maybe right-handed people should play golf left-handed.
- Hold two mid-irons together and gently swing backwards and forwards gradually increasing speed. The process of swinging the extra weight of 2 clubs will make the feeling of swinging one club very light and easy.
- Hold an iron low on the handle and flex your wrists backwards and forwards so that the club-head approaches your shoulders.

How to use your bucket of balls.

Split your bucket of range balls in the following way:

Short Game - ½ the bucket of balls
Mid to Long Irons - ¼ the bucket of balls
Drives - ¼ the bucket of balls

Note:
The range balls may not carry as far as the balls you normally use on the course. For example, at my range the balls carry 10% less according to one coach and 20% less according to another. The former isn't too bad because on the course

we're often playing out of semi-rough grass which takes some distance off the ball anyway. Nevertheless, it is wise to check with the assistant at the range because ball distances can vary a good deal.

Distance/ Direction	Driver	3 Wood	Hybrid	4 Iron	5 Iron	6 Iron	7 Iron	8 Iron	9 Iron	PW	LW	SW
Distance 1												
Direction 1												
Distance 2												
Direction 2												
Distance 3												
Direction 3												
Average Distance												
Average Direction												

The order of practice.

1. The short game including chipping, pitching, bunker shots and putting (the latter is done with your own balls on the putting green normally).
2. The mid and long irons.
3. The driver.

Regular players.

- Always use your pre-shot routine to hit every shot.
- Work on specific drills relating to the different clubs.
- Practise your distance and direction control on the golf range. Use a table to record the results (see the template above). You need to know what average distance you hit

well struck shots for each club in your bag. Use a label on the club's shaft to note the average distance for that club. You'll be surprised at your increased confidence on the course.

- Try to be especially accurate with the 7, 8 and 9 irons as more shots require these clubs on the golf course.

Practise as if playing.

If you play the same course a great deal, then take the scorecard for it to the range (provided it has simple yardage diagrams on it).
Follow the diagrams and imagine you are playing those holes. Choose clubs according to the result of the last shot.

Generally.

- Start with mini-swings and gradually increase them.
- Hit balls with your feet together.
- Take full swings at half power.
- Extend your club head down the target line with a *high* follow through position.
- Grip pressure should be light.
- Hit balls different distances with the same club.

Club distances.

The table below shows average club distances (yards) against swing speeds (listed in bold at the top of the columns). See how they compare against your personally recorded ones.

I found these particularly useful as a starting point. But if you wish to know your distances more accurately, then it would be best to visit a coach who has Trackman or other radar devices. The Trackman will show you things like club head speed, attack angle, club path, ball speed, launch angle, total distance, carry distance, direction and more.

Another way to get to get more accurate knowledge of your distances is to have a friend stand at the side of the range to record them. They can move forwards as distances get longer.

	60	70	80	90	100	110	120	130	140
Driver (Total)	155	181	206	232	258	284	310	335	361
Driver (Carry)	144	168	192	216	240	264	288	312	336
3-Wood	130	152	174	195	217	239	260	282	304
5-Wood	123	144	164	185	205	226	246	267	288
Hybrid	121	141	161	181	201	221	241	261	281
3-Iron	114	133	151	170	189	208	227	246	265
4-Iron	109	127	145	163	181	199	218	236	254
5-Iron	104	121	139	156	173	191	208	225	243
6-Iron	98	114	131	147	163	180	196	212	229
7-Iron	92	108	123	138	154	169	184	200	215
8-Iron	86	100	114	129	143	157	171	186	200
9-Iron	79	93	106	119	132	145	159	172	185
PW	73	85	97	109	121	134	146	158	170

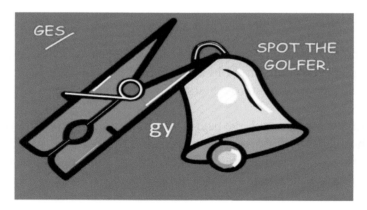

GES

gy

SPOT THE GOLFER.

CURING THE DREADED SLICE WITH THE DRIVER.

I had a terrible slice when using the driver, because I tended to swing out-to-in; but, more importantly, I seemed to be opening the club face at impact.

The cure:

1. The ball – as I was putting slicing spin on the ball, I tried various low spin balls off the tee. The Callaway CXR Control helped me most. It was also very reasonable in price.
2. The tee – I ensured the length of tee I used seated the ball so I could see half of it above the driver head.
3. I made sure that I did not put the ball too far forward in my stance. I played it from halfway between the middle of my stance and my left foot's instep.
4. The shaft – my shaft is "regular" and graphite and I had the feeling that it was twisting at impact. So, at set up, I closed the clubface a little and then adjusted my grip. (I closed my grip a little by moving my left hand slightly round to the right on the grip so I could see three knuckles).
5. As (in my case) the club's head seemed to impact nearer the hosel at impact, I decided to set the middle of the club-head to the inside edge of the ball to allow the sweet spot to make a purer contact (see diagram). You can see the strike position by spraying your club face with something like an athlete's-foot spray.
6. I attempted to approach the ball on a slightly in-to-out path by keeping my right arm closer to my body as I swung down. Now, when I want to fade the ball on purpose, I simply lessen the angle of closure a little bit. An alternative to this was to set the feet positions as for a draw.

TIPS FOR PLAYING THE COURSE.

When in a competition of some kind, the decisions that you make in a round of golf are multiple. Choice of ball, clubs, tees are just the start. A careful study of the course's yardage book or "app" can often help reduce your scores. (Google Earth is useful for this). Also, various forms of measuring distances are available for use on the course. You need to check that you are allowed to use them in competitive situations though. In practice situations, of course, you have the liberty to attempt many different shots and strategies to make improvements to your game, but if you wish to break 100, 90 or 80 then the later tips will help.

As of 2012, the USGA's handicap manual required that holes be measured horizontally with surveying instruments, an electric measuring device or a global positioning system. The measurement of a hole is from the permanent marker (tombstone) on the tee to the middle of the green following the standard path along the fairway.

Some courses have posts at 100yds, 150yds and 200yds (from the centre of the green) on the edge of the fairways. There may be coloured disks at points along the fairway. Generally, the red one is 100yds; the white is 150yds; and the blue one is 200yds.

Decisions.

There will be times you may have to:
play safe,
play strategically or
have a go.

At all times know and play to your strengths. This means you must assess your game honestly. For example, if you hit a 3 fairway wood well and long irons inconsistently then use the wood and slightly lower the position of your grip on the handle instead ("choking down").

In safe play eliminate the hazards as much as possible by considering the directions and accessible distances for you to get to the green without trouble, particularly on long holes. Also, try to leave a short club shot to the green which you can accurately hit nine out of ten times.

On the par 3 holes you may be able to just go for it landing the ball on the green. The right club for distance, air density and wind is a choice that you must get right. Also, take into account the slope up or down to the green. An uphill hole will require going a couple of clubs longer if you're going to reach the green (e.g., a 5 iron instead of the usual 7iron).

A 200 yard drive uphill covers 165 yards only.

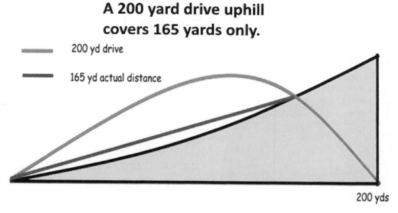

— 200 yd drive

— 165 yd actual distance

200 yds

A downhill one may require a club that is shorter (e.g., a pitching wedge instead of an 8 iron). The more aggressive play on par 4s may well result in errors or, if successful, in birdies. These holes involve hard choices. Below are plans for playing three imaginary holes with simply listed yardages. The yellow tees are the ones selected on this occasion.

HOLE 1: PAR 4: W325 Y310 R295 YDS.

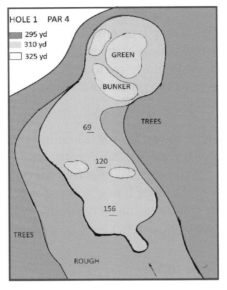

A dogleg right which requires the tee shot to be aimed between the first bunkers. Ideally, 10-20yds past the left one. This leaves a short to mid-iron across the bunker to the green (about 90yds) which is protected on by two bunkers and out of bounds beyond. Alternatively, play short of the bunkers to be safe. Then to a position on the fairway that gives a short, clear shot over the large bunker to the green. The main problem about going for it from before the bunkers is you must clear the large bunker but stop quickly or you will run out of bounds.

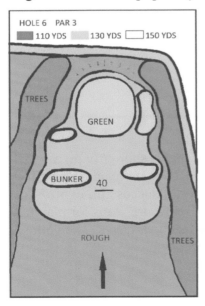

HOLE 6: PAR 3: W150 Y130 R110 YDS.

This is played downhill from an elevated tee. Two large bunkers short of the green and others to the right and left make an accurate shot down the middle important. The green slopes to the back and beyond that the ball will run down a slope to out of bounds. This green remains soft after rain and is difficult to read for putting. It is a hole to birdie so go for it.

HOLE 13: PAR 5: W535 Y491 R475 YDS.

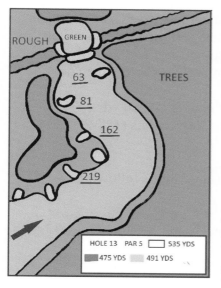

A sharp dogleg left with out of bounds on the left-hand side. A long tee shot (220-260yds) over the marker post will leave a further lay-up shot into the fairway near the two far bunkers 81yds and 63yds from the green. The green is protected by a bunker across the front, but the angle of its front bank is steep. Too much club is best to avoid it. Alternatively, you may want to play safe. So, take two shots to get just beyond the bend. Another towards the gap between the bunkers. This leaves a shorter iron shot to the green. This means you'll be on the green in four shots.

MEASURING PERFORMANCE.

It was Eric Jones (long drive champion and PGA coach) who suggested that golfers assess their performance in a systematic way. I've developed this idea somewhat. The shots that may be measured (listed from the green back to the tee) include:

Putting, Chipping (5-10 yds), Pitching (10-60 yds), Shorter Approaches (60-120 yds), Long Approaches (120-220yds) and Driving.

The **performance** may be measured in the following categories:

Contact, Direction, Distance and Shape.

So, let's take **putting** as an example:

1. Putting contact – Is the face square at impact and on a slight rise to give the ball top spin? Do you know the position of the sweet spot and hit it consistently?
2. Direction – Is the arc of the club swing constant or, if straight back and straight forward is it stable or does it wobble? Does the club point to the hole at the end of the shot?
3. Distance – Does the length or speed of the club swing relate to the distance to be covered consistently. How do you adjust for uphill and downhill putts?
4. Shape – Have you read the borrow? How do you personally assess your aim point to allow for it?

I suggest you answer these questions honestly giving yourself a mark out of ten and if weaknesses are found, then over-practise until they are corrected. This may require you to observe someone like a coach demonstrating the skill involved or finding drills (e.g., on the internet) to promote correct practice.

Stroke	Contact	Direction	Distance	Shape
Putting				
Chipping				
Pitching				
Short Approach				
Long Approach				
Driver				

The same process may be applied to the other shots (although not all measures will apply). The table above may be used for this purpose.

71

EQUIPMENT.

When considering the **purchase of clubs**, there are several variables that need consideration. For example, which clubs? The length, material and flexibility of the shaft, the overall weight, forged or cast club-heads and grip shape and thickness.

Normally a set of golf clubs includes nine irons, three woods, a hybrid and a putter. This makes up the 14 clubs allowed in the bag.

The **bladed iron heads** have a small sweet spot.

The **cavity-back irons** have a larger sweet spot so average golfers can produce longer and straighter shots on off-centre hits.

The woods have a variety of **swing weights** and trial and error alone can show which is most suitable to the golfer. The **lie angle** should fit the swing of the golfer. Manufacturers may use the following measures to assess what's best:

- height of golfer:
- stature; and
- length of arms.

A pro (without radar devices) may do this by:

- Taking a variety of clubs with different lie angles.
- Placing tape across the bottom.
- Get you to hit shots using the right stance – especially in relation to how low your arms drop at address.
  (The above swings strike the ball from a hard board).
- See which club has the tape worn at the centre of the sole. That is the right lie angle for that club.

Tape worn at the toe shows the club is too flat and balls fly right.

Tape worn at the heel shows the angle is too steep and balls fly left.

The lie angle on a forged club head is easier to adjust than a cast club head.

Flex of the shaft.

The right flex of shaft is important for distance and direction of strike. There are four main flexes:
Ladies' - L
Quite flexible - A
Regular men's - R
Stiff men's - S

Again, the best ones are judged by using them and noting their performance for your swing.

Length of shaft.

Generally, there are two measures needed to determine the right length of shaft for a golfer. They are:
1. The golfer's height; and
2. The wrist to ground height.

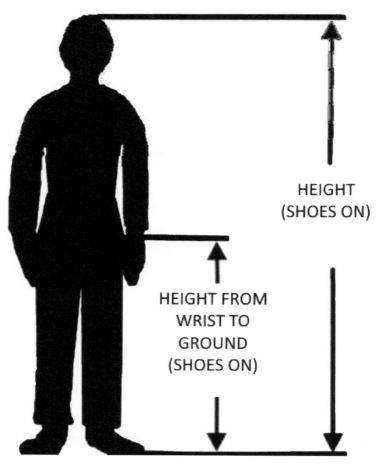

HEIGHT
(SHOES ON)

HEIGHT FROM
WRIST TO
GROUND
(SHOES ON)

Each club has a standard length of shaft as in the Table 1 in Appendix 1 where lengths are also determined from Table 2.

Club grips

The grip on any golf club is important but especially that on the putter. They vary in size, shape and colour, so it is important to decide on the diameter of your grip relative to both performance and comfort. It is, therefore, better to buy them in person rather than by mail order. Even then it is better to find a retailer where you can try them out. Ideally, when the grip is held in the left hand (for a right-handed golfer) near the top of the grip, then the two middle fingers should just touch the heel of the thumb.

In general terms, the grips may be classed as very small, small, standard, large and extra-large. The table below shows the grip needed based on hand size - measuring from the top of the middle finger to the crease where the wrist joins the hand. It also indicates the "Golf Pride" terminology for each in the brackets.

Length in inches	Size of grip
Less than 5	Very small (Junior)
5 to 6.5	Small (Undersize)
6.6 to 7.5	Standard (Standard)
7.6 to 9	Large (Midsize)
9.1 to 10	Extra large (Jumbo)

Maintaining grips.

You can maintain the grips by washing them in a solution of warm water and mild washing-up liquid making sure you rinse well. Then, using a towel, pat them dry. Once dried, they should feel a little tacky.

It is also wise to store the clubs indoors when not in use as the grips are susceptible to changes in temperature. Over time, the grip may lose its "tackiness", become torn at the base or develop cracks. Hence, depending on how regularly you use your clubs, the grips may need to be replaced over one or two years. If you play 3-4 times each week, then it would be best to change the grips on a yearly basis. (Appendix 5 shows how you may change the grip of a club).

Metals.

1.   Softer Zinc and Aluminium heads are inexpensive and okay for beginners.
2.   Softer stainless steels are a good metal for irons. Lie angles may be adjusted easily, and the feel is good.
3.   Harder stainless steels are best for fairway woods creating more compression and distance. They are also good for irons.
5. Titanium is best for drivers.

GES

CAN YOU SPOT THE GOLFER?

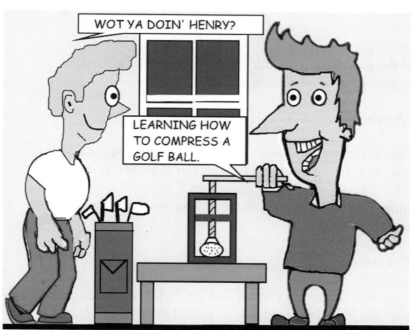

Some Common Formats of Play.

Stroke Play (and Medal Play).

In stroke play the number of strokes taken by an individual is recorded for each hole. (This includes any penalty strokes taken). The number of total strokes taken is calculated at the end of the round to give a final score.

This may be played with the lowest gross score being the winner or, if handicaps are considered, with the lowest nett score being the winner.

If the tournament is described as a "Medal", then every hole must be putted out. There are no "gimmies".

Also, medals are generally played from the back tees ensuring the full length of the course is played, whereas everyday stroke play may be from the yellow tees.

If the tournament includes several rounds of golf, then the lowest total of all rounds wins.

Match Play.

Match play is a format in which the round is played with the aim of winning individual holes. For example, if on the first hole John scores 3 and Paul scores 5, then John wins the hole. The winner is the player who has won most of the eighteen holes.

Foursomes.

This format involves two teams (A and B) each comprising two players. Each player of a team must tee off alternately. One teeing off at the odd-numbered holes and the other teeing off at the even-numbered ones. They then alternate their striking until

78

the ball is holed out. The final scorecard should then show the number of strokes by the team for each of the holes and a total score at the end. The team with the lowest score wins.

Four Ball.

Four ball is also played in teams of two golfers but in this case each team member plays his or her own ball for the entire round. The better of the two team members' scores is recorded for each hole. These scores are added to give a final total. The lower of the two teams' total scores wins if stroke play was decided on; or the highest number of holes wins if match play was decided upon.

Greensomes.

Here we again have two teams (A and B) each having two players. Both players of team A drive off the tee. Team B's players do likewise. Each team decides which of the drives has finished up in the best position and the other balls are picked up. The player who did not do the drive for the best ball takes the next shot. The players then alternate until the ball is holed out. The score is recorded. The team with the lowest total of all holes wins.

Handicaps may also be considered in Greensomes, and the suggested handicap percentages are listed in Appendix 4.

Gruesomes.

Gruesomes are played in the same way as Greensomes with one major differences – each team chooses the ball to be played by their opponents.

COMPLETING A TYPICAL SCORECARD.

Here is a typical scorecard. It is usually completed by an opponent who lists his own score in the "Marker" column and the player's (in this case, in the A column). The player's name would be listed in the row for Player A at the top.

COMPETITION											Please indicate which tees used				
Date			Time				H'cap Index	Course H'cap	Playing H'cap		PAR	CR	SR	✓	
Player A											M	70	68.1	124	☐
Player B											M	70	68.7	119	☐
Marker											F	71	71.4	128	☐
Hole	Marker's Score	White Yards	Yellow Yards	Par	Stroke Index	A	B	Nett Score		Red Yards	Blue Yards	Par	Stroke Index		
1		304	289	4	9					272	173	4	8		
2		277	272	4	7					217	213	4	12		
3		399	383	4	5					286	279	4	14		
4		168	162	3	15					150	141	3	16		
5		439	401	4	1					348	252	4	6		
6		146	125	3	17					110	94	3	18		
7		367	358	4	3					349	268	4	2		
8		149	139	3	11					139	131	3	10		
9		505	502	5	13					454	374	5	4		
		2754	2631	34	OUT					2325	1925	34	OUT		

NOTE: THE AVERAGE ROUND TAKES 3 HRS. 45 MINS.

10		393	377	4	6					333	260	4	13		
11		505	489	5	16					411	335	5	11		
12		339	332	4	10					281	215	4	7		
13		528	486	5	2					470	317	5	1		
14		206	168	3	4					140	134	3	15		
15		371	368	4	12					362	300	4	3		
16		329	329	4	18					326	247	4	5		
17		187	182	3	14					136	132	3	17		
18		418	408	4	8					398	341	5	9		
		3276	3139	36	IN					2857	2281	37	IN		
		2754	2631	34	OUT					2325	1925	34	OUT		
		6030	5770	70	TOTAL					5182	4206	71	TOTAL		

STABLEFORD POINTS OR PAR RESULT?	HANDICAP		Holes won	
	NETT		Holes lost	
			Result	

Marker's Signature _____

Player's Signature _____

The area for "Competition" should be completed e.g., "Seniors' Medal", and the date should be noted along with the tee-time.

In the top right corner, we see course information and the types of tees. Par shows the average number of strokes for a scratch player to complete the course. CR is the course rating. SR is the slope rating for the course.

As the round is a medal, the white tees box should be ticked.

To the left of this area, we see spaces for the Player A's Handicap Index, His Course Handicap, and His Playing Handicap. These are described in detail in Appendix 4.

On the left we see the yardages for each hole from the Yellow and the White tees. On the right we see those for the Red and Blue tees. Those for the white tees would be useful knowledge the competition.

The stroke index column shows the difficulty of achieving PAR on each hole. The first one being 9. This tells us that this is the ninth most difficult hole on the course. Hole 5 has a stroke index of 1 showing us it is the most difficult hole. Hole 18 has a stroke index of 18 showing it is the easiest hole.

As already noted, the marker places his strokes for each hole in the left column. The strokes taken by Player A go in the A Column.

The number of strokes that go in the Nett column are the strokes taken minus the number of strokes his playing handicap allows for that hole. If a player has a playing handicap of 18, then he would be allowed 1 stroke on every hole. If he had a playing handicap of 19, then he would be allowed 2 strokes on the most difficult hole (stroke index 1) and one on the other seventeen. If his playing handicap is 24, then he would be allowed 2 strokes on the six most difficult holes (stroke indexes

1-6) and 1 stroke on the other twelve. However, if his playing handicap is 15, he is allowed 1 stroke on the fifteen most difficult holes and no allowance on the other 3. All the results added together in that column give a final nett score.

In the last column Stableford points may be entered if that system is being played. This process was invented by Dr. Frank Stableford in 1931. Its aim was to speed up play by allowing amateurs to pick up a ball when they could score no further points on a hole. The points were allotted in this way:

Strokes on a hole relative to PAR	Points Allotted
3 under Par (Albatross)	5
2 under Par (Eagle)	4
1 under Par (Birdie)	3
Par	2
1 over Par	1
2 or more over Par	0

Now see if the following makes sense!

COMPETITION	*Seniors' Stableford*					Please indicate which tees used				
Date **11.02.19** Time **8.50**		H'cap Index	Course H'cap	Playing H'cap		PAR	CR	SR	✓	
Player A **J. Cricket**		26.2	27.6	28	M	70	68.1	124	☐	
Player B					M	70	68.1	119	𝕏	
Marker **G. Heavens**		8.0	8.4	8		71	71.8	128	■	

Hole	Marker's Score	White Yards	Yellow Yards	Par	Stroke Index	A	B	Nett Score	✶ ∶ ∶	Red Yards	Blue Yards	Par	Stroke Index
1	4/2	304	289	4	9	6		4	2	272	173	4	8
2	6/1	277	272	4	7	5		3	3	217	213	4	12
3	5/2	399	383	4	5	4		2	4	286	279	4	14
4	4/1	168	162	3	15	4		3	2	150	141	3	16

Once the results have been calculated (under whatever system) the scorecard is double checked by the player and marker and, if correct, it is signed by both.

GOLF: A LESSON FOR CHRISTIANS.

Relative to the Christian life, GOLF might be seen as:

G -   GOD'S
O -   ORDER for
L -   LIFE and
F -   FELLOWSHIP.

The Cost.

Golf comes with a cost. Whether you apply for membership of a club or simply desire to play a round, there is a cost involved. However, God has paid the fee for your salvation, and you may begin the path of life free of charge. It is written in John 3:16: "For God so  loved the world, that he gave his only begotten Son, that whosoever believeth in him should not perish, but have everlasting life."

There is no greater love! God gave His Son to die to save those who were His enemies. He had decreed that the wages of sin is death, and we are all sinners – rebels in the sight of a holy God. In order that God could save us and remain righteous, then sin had to be judged. Hence, He sent His Son to take the punishment that we deserved. Amazing grace!

God has made Him to be sin for us that we might be made the righteousness of God through faith in Him. To avail ourselves of this salvation, we must show repentance towards God and put our faith in His Son. Initially, we must acknowledge before God in prayer that we deserved nothing but judgment and tell Him we accept the sacrifice of His Son on our behalf.

The hymnwriter, Albert Midlane (1825-1909) put it this way:

1 The perfect righteousness of God
is witnessed in the Saviour's blood;
'Tis the cross of Christ we trace
His righteousness, yet wondrous grace.

2 God could not pass the sinner by;
Justice demands that he should die;
But in the cross of Christ we see
How God can save, yet righteous be.

3 The judgment fell on Jesus' head;
'Twas in His blood sin's debt was paid;
Stern Justice can demand no more,
And Mercy can dispense her store.

4 The sinner who believes is free,
Can say, "The Saviour died for me";
Can point to the atoning blood
And say, "This made my peace with God."

Those who implicitly trust their lives to Christ know the judgment for their sin has passed and that they have eternal life (1 John 5:13). They know that they have been spiritually born again and that the Holy Spirit indwells them (John 1:11-14). Furthermore, they know their destination is Heaven.

The apostle Peter wrote: "Forasmuch as ye know that ye were not redeemed with corruptible things, *as* silver and gold, from your vain conversation *received* by tradition from your fathers; but with the precious blood of Christ, as of a lamb without blemish and without spot..." Salvation cannot be bought with silver and gold, neither can it be obtained by so-called good works (Ephesians 2:8-9). It can only be by grace (**G**od's

Redemption At Christ's Expense) through faith. Not one in heaven will be able to boast: "I got here my way!"

The Tee – The First Step.

As we stand on the tee, we look forward to decide upon our first shot. It reminds us of the verse that says: "Let us run with patience the race that is set before us, looking unto Jesus the author and finisher of our faith…" Our focus as believers is upon Christ. He walked a perfect pathway upon earth and suffered more than we can know. Therefore, we may be encouraged  to look to heaven with the eyes of faith and see Him crowned with glory and honour. Our pathway leads that way. So let us walk in love, even as He did, until we finish our course (Ephesians 5:2).

The Fairway – Keep to the Path.

As golfers, we know the benefits of staying on the fairway. We also know how difficult that is. In John 14:6 we find the way that leads to a relationship with God as our Father: "Jesus saith unto him, I am the way, the truth, and the life: no man cometh unto the Father, but by me." (Christianity is not so much a religion, but a relationship with God).

There is a way that seems right to an unbelieving man, but the scripture tells us it results in death (Proverbs 14:12). The Lord Jesus Christ spoke of two ways in Matthew 7:13-14: "Enter ye in at the strait gate: for wide *is* the gate, and broad *is* the way, that leadeth to destruction, and many there be which go in thereat: because strait *is* the gate, and narrow *is* the way, which leadeth unto life, and few there be that find it."

Christians are on the way to life – the fair way! It is a life lived in relationship with their God and Father and His Son. As 1 John 1:1-3 states: "That which was from the beginning, which we have heard, which we have seen with our eyes, which we have looked upon, and our hands have handled, of the Word of life; (for the life was manifested, and we have seen *it*, and bear witness, and shew unto you that eternal life, which was with the Father, and was manifested unto us;) that which we have seen and heard declare we unto you, that ye also may have fellowship with us: and truly our fellowship *is* with the Father, and with his Son Jesus Christ." Not only do Christians enjoy this fellowship, but they enjoy the fellowship of others of the same mind. A very special camaraderie indeed!

The Rough – Trials!

If you play golf as I do, then you will find yourself in the rough quite often. It is then a question of escape! In Christianity, the rough represents trials. We read in 1 Peter 1:7: "That the trial of your faith, being much more precious than of gold that perisheth,

though it be tried with fire, might be found unto praise and honour and glory at the appearing of Jesus Christ..."

There are many trials the Christian passes through in life. But the Lord always provides a way of escape. In 1 Corinthians 10:13 the apostle Paul states: "There hath no temptation (trial) taken you, but such as is common to man: but God *is* faithful, who will not suffer you to be tempted (tested) above that ye are able; but will with the temptation (trial) also make a way to escape, that ye may be able to bear *it*." The way of escape from trials is obedience to God. Christ who was tried by the devil in the wilderness overcame him by correctly quoting scripture. The Lord was tested in spirit, soul and body but always remained obedient to His Father.

Furthermore, the Lord accompanies us as we pass through trials just as he did with Shadrach, Meshach and Abednego in the fiery furnace. We read in Daniel 3:24-25: "Then Nebuchadnezzar the king was astonied, and rose up in haste, *and* spake, and said unto his counsellors, Did not we cast three men bound into the midst of the fire? They answered and said unto the king, True, O king. He answered and said, Lo, I see four men loose, walking in the midst of the fire, and they have no hurt; and the form of the fourth is like the Son of God."

Trees and Shrubs – Afflictions.

Trees and shrubs are two of the worst hazards on the golf course. It is almost always a case of playing the simplest shot or, if possible, taking a penalty to be free of them. In this article, they represent afflictions that the Christian may face. It may be a question of enduring them or adapting to them. In Romans 8:26 we read: "Likewise the Spirit also helpeth our infirmities: for we know not what we should pray for as we ought..."

Sometimes, we are in physical pain or limited by some kind of ailment. We may be lame, blind, deaf or dumb. Furthermore, circumstances may bring sorrows and burdens. Paul prayed three times concerning an affliction he had (probably a failure of sight). We hear him saying in 2 Corinthians 12:8-10: "For this thing I besought the Lord thrice, that it might depart from me. And he said unto me, My grace is sufficient for thee: for my strength is made perfect in weakness. Most gladly therefore will I rather glory in my infirmities, that the power of Christ may rest upon me. Therefore I take pleasure in infirmities, in reproaches, in necessities, in persecutions, in distresses for Christ's sake: for when I am weak, then am I strong."

The Lord's reply to Paul changed his whole attitude to afflictions. He realised that even afflictions were allowed by the God who loved him and sought the best for him.

Joni Eareckson was paralysed from the shoulders down following a diving accident. This led to her trusting in the Lord. She has continued with Him ever since and remains a true and faithful servant. One of her books, "Joni" is a memorable read!

I, personally, knew a Christian woman who, upon hearing she had breast cancer, prayed to the Lord (with sobs) thanking Him for it. She had the faith to see that all things work together for good to those who love God and are called according to His purpose (Romans 8:28). That woman passed on. Her soul went to be with her Lord (2 Corinthians 5:8) where she consciously awaits that glorious day when she shall receive her new body (1 Corinthians 15:35-46).

Water Hazards – Chastening.

There is little we can do as golfers should we find our balls have splashed into water. We simply must take our punishment, regaining the ball with the required penalty.

In the Christian experience our communion with God is to be sustained. However, we often fail Him. As our God and Father, He will chasten us if we go on sinning. In Hebrews 12:6 we find: "For whom the Lord loveth he chasteneth, and scourgeth every son whom he receiveth." If we say we are believers and are not chastened by the Father, then we are not  among His children. We are classed as illegitimate. To avoid chastening, it is wise to keep short accounts with God. When we do sin, we should immediately confess it to Him directly, knowing that He is faithful and just to forgive us our sins (1 John 1:9).

Bunkers – Snares.

Bunkers are man-made. They are snares which attempt to stop us reaching our goal. The attitude of this psalmist ought to be ours - "The wicked have laid a snare for me: yet I erred not from thy precepts" (Psalm 119:110). Knowing and obeying the will of God will  help us to overcome the traps that wicked men may set for us. We may be assured that God will act behind the scenes. You can read the book of Esther to see this. In the death of Haman in that book, we see the truth of Proverbs 26:27: "Whoso diggeth a pit shall fall therein: and he that rolleth a stone, it will return upon him."

As Christians, we are obey the Christ who said: "…Love your enemies, bless them that curse you, do good to them that hate you, and pray for them which despitefully use you, and persecute you" (Matthew 5:44).

The Green – the Victory.

What a joy it is to achieve our goal - to reach the green. As far as Christians are concerned, Psalm 98:1 expresses the feeling relating to this achievement and gives the credit to God: "A Psalm. O sing unto the LORD a new song; for he hath done marvellous things: his right hand, and his holy arm, hath gotten him the victory." God has been with us all the way home. We will dwell in the place (in the Father's house) which has been prepared by the Lord Jesus. John 14:1-3 reads: "Let not your heart be troubled: ye believe in God, believe also in me. In my Father's house are many mansions: if *it were* not *so*, I would have told you. I go to prepare a place for you. And if I go and prepare a place for you, I will come again, and receive you unto myself; that where I am, *there* ye may be also."

The Prize – the Reward.

The winning golfer may receive a prize after his round, but all Christians will reach heaven and there receive rewards for their service for God in this life. The reward will be according to the work done (2 Corinthians 5:10; 1 Corinthians 12:11-15).

APPENDIX 1: FINDING THE CORRECT SHAFT LENGTH.

The adjustments of shaft lengths based on wrist to ground and height of golfer measures may be determined from the tables below:

Clubs	Steel Shafted Irons	Graphite Shafted Irons
	Male & Female	Male & Female
Driver	43 1/2" & 42 1/2"	44" & 43"
3 Wood	42 1/2" & 41 1/2"	43" & 42"
5 Wood	41 1/2" & 40 1/2"	42" & 41"
1 Iron	39 1/2" & 38 1/2"	40" & 39"
2 Iron	39" & 38"	39 1/2" & 38 1/2"
3 Iron	38 1/2" & 37 1/2"	39" & 38"
4 Iron	38" & 37"	38 1/2" & 37 1/2"
5 Iron	37 1/2" & 36 1/2"	38" & 37"
6 Iron	37" & 36"	37 1/2" & 36 1/2"
7 Iron	36 1/2" & 35 1/2"	37" & 36"
8 Iron	36" & 35"	36 1/2" & 35 1/2"
9 Iron	35 1/2" & 34 1/2"	36" & 35"
PW, AW, SW, LW	35" & 34"	35 1/2" & 34 1/2"

Wrist to Floor Length	Your Height								
	4' 10" - 5' 0"	5' 0" - 5' 2"	5' 2" - 5' 4"	5' 4" - 5' 7"	5' 7" - 6' 0"	6' 0" - 6' 2"	6' 2" - 6' 4"	6' 4" - 6' 7"	6' 7" - 6' 9"
40"	+ 2 1/4"	+ 2 1/4"	+ 2 1/4"	+ 2"	+ 2"	+ 2"	+ 1 3/4"	+ 1 3/4"	+ 1 1/2"
39 1/2"	+ 2"	+ 2"	+ 2"	+ 1 3/4"	+ 1 3/4"	+ 1 3/4"	+ 1 1/2"	+ 1 1/2"	+ 1 1/2"
39"	+ 2"	+ 2"	+ 2"	+ 1 3/4"	+ 1 3/4"	+ 1 3/4"	+ 1 1/2"	+ 1 1/2"	+ 1 1/2"
38 1/2"	+ 1 1/2"	+ 1 1/2"	+ 1 1/2"	+ 1 1/2"	+ 1 1/2"	+ 1 1/2"	+ 1"	+ 1"	+ 1"
38"	+ 1 1/2"	+ 1 1/2"	+ 1 1/2"	+ 1"	+ 1"	+ 1"	+ 1"	+ 1"	+ 1"
37 1/2"	+ 1"	+ 1"	+ 1"	+ 1"	+ 1"	+ 1"	+ 1/2"	+ 1/2"	+ 1/2"
37"	+ 1"	+ 1"	+ 1"	+ 1/2"	+ 1/2"	+ 1/2"	+ 1/2"	+ 1/2"	+ 1/2"
36 1/2"	+ 1/2"	+ 1/2"	+ 1/2"	+ 1/2"	+ 1/2"	+ 1/2"	+ 1/4"	+ 1/4"	+ 1/4"
36"	+ 1/2"	+ 1/2"	+ 1/2"	+ 1/4"	+ 1/4"	+ 1/4"	+ 1/4"	+ 1/4"	+ 1/4"
35 1/2"	+ 1/4"	+ 1/4"	+ 1/4"	+ 1/4"	+ 1/4"	+ 1/4"	STD	STD	STD
35"	+ 1/4"	+ 1/4"	+ 1/4"	STD	STD	STD	STD	STD	STD
34 1/2"	STD	STD	STD	STD	STD	STD	- 1/4"	- 1/4"	- 1/4"
34"	STD	STD	STD	- 1/4"	- 1/4"	- 1/4"	- 1/4"	- 1/4"	- 1/4"
33 1/2"	- 1/4"	- 1/4"	- 1/4"	- 1/4"	- 1/4"	- 1/4"	- 1/2"	- 1/2"	- 1/2"
33"	- 1/4"	- 1/4"	- 1/4"	- 1/2"	- 1/2"	- 1/2"	- 1/2"	- 1/2"	- 1/2"
32 1/2"	- 1/2"	- 1/2"	- 1/2"	- 1/2"	- 1/2"	- 1/2"	- 3/4"	- 3/4"	- 3/4"
32"	- 1/2"	- 1/2"	- 1/2"	- 3/4"	- 3/4"	- 3/4"	- 3/4"	- 3/4"	- 3/4"
31 1/2"	- 3/4"	- 3/4"	- 3/4"	- 3/4"	- 3/4"	- 3/4"	- 1"	- 1"	- 1"
31"	- 3/4"	- 3/4"	- 3/4"	- 1"	- 1"	- 1"	- 1"	- 1"	- 1"
30 1/2"	- 1"	- 1"	- 1"	- 1"	- 1"	- 1"	- 1 1/4"	- 1 1/4"	- 1 1/4"
30"	- 1"	- 1"	- 1"	- 1 1/4"	- 1 1/4"	- 1 1/4"	- 1 1/4"	- 1 1/4"	- 1 1/4"
29 1/2"	- 1 1/4"	- 1 1/4"	- 1 1/4"	- 1 1/4"	- 1 1/4"	- 1 1/4"	- 1 1/2"	- 1 1/2"	- 1 1/2"
29"	- 1 1/4"	- 1 1/4"	- 1 1/4"	- 1 1/2"	- 1 1/2"	- 1 1/2"	- 1 1/2"	- 1 1/2"	- 1 1/2"

APPENDIX 2: SOME IMPORTANT RULE CHANGES FROM 2019.

- Three minutes are allowed to search for a ball.
- You may replace a ball which was moved as you looked for it – without penalty.
- If the ball is plugged anywhere on the course, except the bunker, a free drop is allowed.
- A "club length" is to be defined as the longest club in the bag except for the putter.
- Drops are to be made from knee height.
- If the ball is found on the wrong green, it must be dropped away from the green (no nearer your object hole) so the stance is clear of that green.
- Hitting yourself or your equipment with your ball does not incur a penalty.
- A double hit does not incur a penalty stroke (unless clearly intended).
- In the bunker, incidental touching of the sand is allowed but not when addressing the ball.
- Loose impediments may be moved in bunkers and hazards.
- Any ball in the bunker which is deemed unplayable may be dropped behind the bunker (away from the hole) for two penalty strokes or, alternatively, it may be dropped in the bunker (no nearer the hole) for a penalty of one stroke.
- Water hazards are now classed in the same way as red or yellow hazards.
- The club may be grounded in hazards (except bunkers) and in the water.
- If a ball that has been previously marked on the green moves when addressed, it may be replaced without penalty.
- A ball accidentally moved with a part of your body or equipment may be replaced without penalty.

- Damage on the green on your line of putt may be repaired (within reason).
- The club may not be laid on the green to help the golfer to align his stance.
- Caddies cannot help the golfer to align his putt.
- If the flag is hit while putting on the green, there is no penalty.
- If the ball rests against the flag with part of it below the lip of the hole it is classed as "in the hole".

APPENDIX 3: SPOT THE GOLFER ANSWERS.

Page 4:	Doug Sanders
Page 7:	Nick Faldo
Page 15:	Bobby Locke
Page 23:	Paul Casey ("Popeye")
Page 35	Caroline Masson
Page 39:	Brittany Lang
Page 37:	Billy Horshcel
Page 44:	Gill Morgan
Page 48:	Fred Couples
Page 59:	Inbee Park
Page 64:	Peggy Bell
Page 76:	Justin Rose
Page 94:	Doug Ford

OTHERS.

Page 13:	Backswing
Page 15:	Adam Scott
Page 16:	Rickie Fowler
Page 18:	**HIT THE HOLE SOLUTION.**

APPENDIX 4: THE WHS 2020 HANDICAPPING SYSTEM.

1. The **Handicap Index** provides a measure of your playing ability on a course of standard playing difficulty.

2. The **Course Rating** indicates the typical number of strokes a scratch golfer – generally, meaning a zero-handicap player – will take under normal conditions. Typically, courses have ratings from the high 60s to the middle 70s. It is set by the golfing authority and revised every 10 years.

A particularly tough course could have a par of 72 and a rating from the back tees of 74.3. An easier course would likely have a rating from their back tees that is lower than par.

3. The course's **Slope Rating** measures a course's difficulty relative to a "bogey player" - someone who will carry a course handicap of 20 on a course of standard difficulty. A course of average difficulty carries a slope rating of 113.

The Handicap Index.

Ideally, the **Handicap Index** is calculated by averaging the 8 best handicap differentials of the most recent 20 rounds whether played in competition or generally.

So, it is calculated by averaging the best 8 score differentials out of the most recent 20 *within your scoring record.*

For example:

Player's Name	Henry Roscoe

Course Rating	Slope Rating	Adjusted Gross	Score (Handicap) Differential
72.5	**130**	**82**	**8.3**
72.5	130	95	19.6
72.5	130	91	16.1
72.5	130	91	16.1
72.5	130	90	15.1
72.5	**130**	**89**	**14.3**
72.5	130	92	17.0
72.5	130	101	24.8
72.5	**130**	**87**	**12.6**
72.5	130	94	18.7
72.5	130	93	17.8
72.5	**130**	**88**	**13.5**
72.5	130	94	18.7
72.5	130	91	16.1
72.5	**130**	**83**	**9.1**
72.5	**130**	**88**	**13.5**
72.5	130	94	18.7
72.5	**130**	**87**	**12.6**
72.5	130	92	17.0
72.5	**130**	**83**	**9.1**

The average of Henry's best 8 from his last 20 scores is 93. 0 ÷8. This is 11.6. So, his Handicap Index is 11.6.

If his record did not have 20 scores on it already, a modified calculation will be carried out to provide him with a Handicap Index. The below table highlights how this will be done:

97

Number of score differentials	The score differentials to be used	Adjustment
3	Lowest one	-2
4	Lowest one	-1
5	Lowest one	0
6	Av. of lowest 2	-1
7 or 8	Av. of lowest 2	0
9 or 11	Av. of lowest 3	0
12 or 14	Av. of lowest 4	0
15 or16	Av. of lowest 5	0
17 or 18	Av. of lowest 6	0
19	Av. of lowest 7	0
20	Av. of lowest 8	0

The equation for calculating a **Handicap Differential (HD)** is the Adjusted Gross Score (AGS) minus the Course rating (CR), multiplied by 113, and divided by the Slope Rating (SR).

$$HD = \frac{(AGS - CR) \times 113}{SR}$$

Example:
If my adjusted gross score for 18 holes is 95 and the course rating is 70 and the slope rating for the course was set at 115 then the Handicap Differential would be:

$$\frac{(95 - 70) \times 113}{115} = \frac{25 \times 113}{115} = 24.57$$

The "Gross Score" (number of strokes) of the round may be adjusted if there are any very poor scores on a particular hole. For example, if I scored 10 on a par 4 hole where I would have received 1 stroke (on my present handicap) then the adjusted gross score for the hole would be 4 for the par +

2 standard bogey shots + the 1 stroke I would have received anyway. So, the adjusted gross would be 4+2+1 =7 (not 10).

Again, if I scored 10 on a par 5 hole where I would have received 2 strokes, then the adjusted score would be 5 + 2 bogey shots + the 2 strokes I would have received. The adjusted gross score for the hole would be 5 + 2 + 2 = 9 (not 10).

The Course Handicap.

To calculate your Course Handicap for a social round you need just one calculation:

Handicap Index x (Slope Rating÷113) = Course Handicap

Playing Handicap.

A Playing Handicap provides players with the number of strokes needed based on the course and the *format of play.* To calculate your Playing Handicap for a competitive round you need just one calculation:

Playing Handicap = Course Handicap x Handicap Allowance (i.e., percentage allowed).

See the table below for the set Handicap Allowances for various playing formats

The Playing Handicap is adjusted according to the slope rating of the course you are playing. The slope rating is a measure of how difficult the course is to play.

Any difference between the course rating and par is factored in (For example if the course rating is 72 and par is 71). The applicable Handicap Allowance for your playing format is also applied.

Percentage Handicap Allowances.

The following table sets out the recommended handicap allowances based on medium-sized field events.

Format of Play	Type of Round	Recommended *Handicap Allowance*
Stroke play	Individual	95%
	Individual Stableford	95%
	Individual Par/Bogey	95%
	Individual Maximum Score	95%
	Four-Ball	85%
	Four-Ball Stableford	85%
	Four-Ball Par/Bogey	90%
Match play	Individual	100%
	Four-Ball	90%
Other	Foursomes	50% of combined team handicap
	Greensomes	60% low handicap + 40% high handicap
	Pinehurst/Chapman	60% low handicap + 40% high handicap
	Best 1 of 4 stroke play	75%
	Best 2 of 4 stroke play	85%
	Best 3 of 4 stroke play	100%
	All 4 of 4 stroke play	100%
	Scramble (4 players)	25%/20%/15%/10% from lowest to highest handicap
	Scramble (2 players)	35% low/15% high
	Total score of 2 match play	100%
	Best 1 of 4 Par/Bogey	75%
	Best 2 of 4 Par/Bogey	80%
	Best 3 of 4 Par/Bogey	90%
	4 of 4 Par/Bogey	100%

APPENDIX 5: REPLACING A GOLF CLUB'S GRIP.

To replace a club's grip, you will need the items listed below.

The new grip. A sharp knife preferably with changeable blades. (A hooked blade is ideal for removing the old grip). A heat gun or hair dryer would be useful. Double sided tape about 5 cms wide. Scissors. A marker pen. A bottle of solvent (preferably, odourless). Paper towels. A tray. A vice.

Steps:
1. You simply place the hooked blade underneath the base of the club's old grip and, pushing it away from you, slice it.
2. Peel off the grip.
3. Heat the old tape using the heat gun (or hair dryer), turning the club as you do so.
4. Peel off the old tape. (Any remaining, carefully scrape off with a sharp blade).
5. Lay the club down in the vice. (To protect the shaft, wrap part of the old grip around the area to be clamped).
6. Clamp it carefully in position with the clubhead pointing vertically upwards.
7. Place the new grip against its proposed position on the shaft.
8. Mark the shaft at the bottom of the grip.
9. Place the unsealed sticky side of the tape where the new grip will go starting a quarter of an inch short of the mark made on the shaft and leaving about a half-an-inch extra at the top end. Cut with scissors.
10. Remove the non-sticky sealing strip from the tape and wrap it round the shaft.
11. Working over the tray, take the new grip and, holding your thumb over the end hole partly fill it with solvent.
12. Ensure all the inside is covered with solvent by tipping and turning it.

13. Pour the solvent from the grip over the tape on the shaft (to lubricate it).
14. Push on the new grip in one quick and aggressive movement until you feel the end of the club firmly against the end of the grip.
15. Immediately ensure everything is squared up.
16. Use the paper towels to dry of the grip and your hands.
17. Hold the club in a normal stance to make sure all is well.
18. Leave the club to dry overnight before using it.

Note: if you don't have a vice, you can place the clubhead on the floor jammed between your feet.

GLOSSARY.

A

Alignment: the position of the feet, hips and shoulders in relation to the target.

Angle of Attack: the angle at which the club's head approaches the ball at impact.

Approach Shot: the shot hit towards an accessible green.

B

Backswing: the motion in taking the club away from the ball and setting it in the top position pointing it to the target.

Backspin: the rotational movement of the ball produced by contact with the clubface (usually as it comes down on the ball).

Baseball Grip: a grip in which the hands grip the club independently one above the other.

Birdie: one under par for a hole.

Bladed (Skulled) Shot: a shot where the top half of the ball is struck with the bottom part of an iron.

Bogey: one over par on a hole.

Borrow: the amount a player allows for when hitting a putt on a sloping green.

Break: the amount a putt will curve to the side because of the slope, grain or wind.

Bump and Run: a shot near the green in which the player pitches the ball so that it will run on after the first bounce.

Bunker: usually a sand-filled hollow acting as a trap.

C

Caddie: a person hired to carry clubs and provide some assistance.

Carry: the distance a ball will fly in the air before landing.

Casting: an uncocking of the wrists prematurely resulting in an out to in path.

Cavity-back: an iron in which the back of the club-head is hollowed out.

Centrifugal Force: the force that pulls the club-head outward and downward.

Chip and Run: a shot with little flight and a longer run.

Choke Down: gripping down on the shaft.

Chunk: hitting the turf well behind the ball.

Cleek: a fairway wood that produces high shots.

Closed Clubface: the position formed when the toe of the club is further forward than the heel at address or impact.

Closed Grip: both hands are turned away from the target with the left showing three to four knuckles.

Closed Stance: when the rear foot is pulled back away from the target line.

Cocked Wrists: the hinging motion of the wrists during the backswing.

Compression: the measure of the relative hardness of a golf ball allowing it squash and spring at impact.

Cross-Handed: a grip in which the left (or lead) hand is placed below the right hand.

Cupped Wrist: a position in which the left or top hand is hinged outward at the top of the backswing.

Cut Shot: a shot that fades.

D

Divot: a piece of turf displaced when the club strikes the ball on a descending path.

Double Bogey: score of two over par on a hole.

Double Eagle (or Albatross): a score of three under par on a hole.

Dormie: the point in match play when a player is up in a match by the same number of holes that remain.

Downswing: the forward swing from the top of the backswing.

Draw: a shot which flies slightly from right to left.

E

Eagle: two-under-par on a hole.

Effective Loft: the actual loft on a club at impact.

Extension: the width of the complete swing

F

Fade: a shot that flies slightly from left to right.

Fat Shot: a shot when the club-head strikes the turf behind the ball.

Flange: the sole of a club like a sand wedge or putter.

Flier: a shot from the rough or in wet conditions where the ball flies lower and further than usual.

Flip Shot: a wedge shot that uses a wristy swing to hit the ball a short distance but with a lot of height.

Flop Shot: a flip shot with a longer, slower swing.

Follow-through: the part of the swing that occurs after impact.

Forward Press: a slight movement of the hands forwards starting the swing.

G

Grain: the direction the blades of grass grow on the greens.

Greenkeeper: the course's superintendent.

Grip: the positioning of the hands on the club. There are three main ways: the baseball grip, the overlapping grip and the interlocking grip.

Grooves: the horizontal, scored lines on the face of the clubface.

H

Half Shot: a shot played with a limited backswing swing and reduced swing speed.

Heel: the part of the club-head nearest the hosel (where the shaft joins the head).

Hooding: the placing of the hands ahead of the ball at address and impact.

Hook: a shot that curves sharply from right to left for right-handed players.

Hosel: the part of the club connecting the shaft to the club-head.

I

Impact: the moment the club strikes the ball.

Inside-to-In: the path of the swing where the club-head travels from inside the target line, to impact, and then back inside the target line.

Inside-to-Out: a swing path where the club-head approaches the ball from inside the target line and, after impact, continues to the outside of the target line.

L

Lag: the "trailing" or "following" of the club-head behind the hands on the downswing.

Lag putt or Shot: one that is left short of the target on purpose.

Level-Par: a score of even par.

Lie: the position of the ball when it has come to rest

Lie of the Club-Head: the angle of the sole of the club-head flat on the ground relative to the shaft.

Line of Putt: the intended path of the ball.

Line of Flight: the path taken by the ball

Links: a course formed from land reclaimed from the ocean.

Lob Shot: a short, high shot, usually played with a wedge.

Loft: the degree of angle on the clubface.

Long Irons: the 1-4 irons.

M

Middle or Mid-irons: the 5-7 irons.

Mulligan: in friendly games, hitting a second ball (after a poor stroke) without penalty.

N

Nassau: a competition in which points are awarded for winning the front nine, back nine and the overall eighteen.

O

Offset: the distance between the leading edge of the hosel and the leading edge of the clubface.

One-Piece Takeaway: the beginning of the backswing when the hands, arms and wrists move away from the ball, maintaining the triangle they had at address.

Open Clubface: the heel of the club-head leading the toe.

Open Grip: the hands are turned counterclockwise on the handle of the club.

Open Stance: When the left or lead foot is pulled back farther from the target line than the rear foot.

Outside-to-In: the path of the club-head approaching the ball from outside the target line continuing to the inside of that line following impact.

P

Paddle Grip: a putting grip with a flat surface where the thumbs rest.

Par: Professional Average Result. The score a player with a scratch (0) handicap is expected to make on a hole.

Path: the direction the club travels during a stroke.

Pendulum Stroke: a putting stroke where the club moves back and forth on a constant line. The length of the swing being adjusted to the distance from the target.

Pitch-and-Run: a shot where the ball carries in the air for a short distance before running towards the target.

Plumb-bob: a method for assessing the break of a ball when putting.

Plugged Lie: a lie where the ball has sunk deeply in sand or soft turf.

Pre-Shot Routine: the actions of a player as he addresses the ball.

Pronation: an inward rotation of the hands towards the body's centreline during a stroke.

Pulled Hook: a shot that starts towards the left side of the target line and continues to curve away from that target.

Pulled Shot: a relatively straight shot that begins to the side of the target and flies straight.

Punch Shot: a low-flying shot played with an abbreviated backswing and finish.

Pushed Hook: a shot that begins to the right side of the target but curves back across to the left of the target.

Pushed Shot: a shot that starts to the side of the target and never curves back.

Pushed Slice: a shot that starts to the right side of the target and curves further away.

R

Radius: the distance between the base of the neck and the hands on the grip.

Reading the Green : the process used to judge the break and path of a putt.

Release: the flow of the arms and body through impact with the ball.

Rhythm: the coordination of movement during the golf swing or putting stroke.

S

Setup: the process of addressing the ball so that the club and body are properly aligned.

Shank: the ball is struck from the hosel of the club, usually sending it shooting off to the right.

Shape: to curve a shot to fit the situation on the course.

Short Game: a description of the shots played on and close to the green.

Short Irons: the 8 and 9 irons and wedges.

Slice: A ball flight that curves from left to right to a greater degree than a fade.

Sole: the bottom of a club.

Splash Shot: a shot played from the bunker where the club "splashes" through the sand.

Stance: the position of the feet at address.

Stroke (Medal) Play: a form of competition based on the cumulative number of strokes taken.

Strong Grip: a grip in which the hands are turned counter-clockwise on the grip.

Supination: an outward rotation of the hands away from the body's centreline.

Swaying: an exaggerated lateral movement of the body

Sweet Spot: the point on the clubface where, if it is struck with an object, the clubface will not twist to either side.

Swing Plane: an imaginary surface that describes the path and angle of the club during the swing.

T

Takeaway: the movement of the club at the start of the backswing.

Target Line: a line drawn behind and through the ball to the target.

Tee Box: the area where players start a hole.

Tempo: the speed of the swing.

Texas Wedge: using a putter from off the green.
Timing: the sequence of motions in the golf swing.
Toed Shot: any shot hit off the toe of the club.
Topped Shot: a shot off the bottom of the club which strikes the top half of the ball.
Touch: a player's sense of feel.
Trajectory: the height and angle the ball in flight.
Transition: the change from the backswing to the forward swing.
U
Upright: a steeper-than-normal swing plane.
V
Visualization: a mental image of the shot
W
Waggle: movement of the club designed to keep a player relaxed at address.
Weak Grip: a grip where the hands are turned to the left for a righthanded player.
Whiff: A complete miss.
Y
Yips: nervous tension causing errors in pitching, chipping or putting.

BIBLIOGRAPHY

Some of the books to which the author referred in his research.

RUNYAN, Paul: "The Short Way to Lower Scoring": Golf Digest/Tennis, 1979: ISBN:0914178598 (ISBN 13: 9780914178590).

HOGAN, BEN (WITH WIND, HERBERT): "Five Lessons. The Modern Fundamentals of Golf"; Simon and Schuster UK Ltd; 2006. ISBN 13: 978-0-7432-9528-4.

HOWE, COLIN: "Play Better Golf", Quercus Editions Ltd, 2009. ISBN: 978-84724-646-2.

MEADOWS, CHRIS (WITH RICHARDSON, ALLEN): "Lowering Your Golf Handicap": Parragon, Queen St. House, Bath, UK. ISBN: 978-1-4075-7985-6.

NEWSHAM, GAVIN: "Go Golf": Dorling Kindersley Ltd., 80 Strand, London, 2006. ISBN: 978-1-4053-6320-4.

SOME OF THE MANY VIDEO SITES TO WHICH THE AUTHOR REFERRED FOR RESEARCH.

BALLARD, Clay at Top Speed Golf (https://topspeedgolf.com)

BAZALGETTE, Adam: Scratch Golf Academy (https://scratchgolfacademy.com/free-lessons)

SHIELS, Rick at Rick Shiels Golf (https://www.facebook.com/rickshielspga/videos)

WILSON, Paul at Ignition Golf (https://ignitiongolf.com)

QUINTON Chuck, Rotary Swing Golf (https://rotaryswing.com)

MAUD, Danny: Golf Lessons (https://www.greatgolfvideos.com/pgapro/danny-maude)

HALL, Martin: Revolution Golf. https://www.golfchannel.com/instruction

PELTZ, Dave: Peltzgolf.com. Searches: "Dave Peltz Perfect Putting" or "The Secret Of Every Great Putter".

RUNYAN, Paul: Search: "The Short Way To Lower Scores 01 Putting and Chipping".

JONES, Eric: https://ericjonesgolf.com

COMPACT DISC.

MICKELSON, Phil; "Secrets of the Short Game": Pasea LLC, 2009.

INDEX.

114

THE AUTHOR.

George Stevens was born and educated in the West Country, England. He, later, trained to be a Junior School teacher with Art as his main subject.

His many years of teaching experience included time spent in Northumberland and Suffolk.

Throughout his career, he produced plays and sketches for children to perform. Upon retirement, he took to writing books for children, often relating to his Christian beliefs. He has also written well over 4000 hymns and some Bible-based books for older people.

A few years after retirement, George took up golf as a pastime. He classes each round as "a walk to some purpose". He also finds it an enjoyable way to keep relatively fit.

This book contains the results of some of his research into playing the game. Now over seventy, he wishes he had the strength and flexibility to play better.

EXTRA! EXTRA!
MORE BOOKS BY THE SAME AUTHOR.

"The Adventures of the Red Rubber Ball."
ISBN: 978-0-9557881-0-9
The ordinary life of a young lad called George is changed into one of suspense and adventure when he comes into possession of a red rubber ball that seems to possess special powers. It's story that grips the imagination! Young primary school children love it!

"The Maiden Voyage of the Falcon."

ISBN: 978-0-9557881-1-6
This is a fictional adventure about a teenager sailing on a nineteenth century clipper ship. It is full of excitement where drunkenness, murder, mutiny and danger are met by the overruling mercy of God. The book bears a Christian bias and is written for children between the ages of about eight and twelve years.

"Bah! Humbug!"
ISBN: 978-0-9557881-2-3
This is a play written for children between 9 and 12 years of age. It is an adaptation of "A Christmas Carol" by Charles Dickens. It has been used successfully as a Christmas production in primary schools. It is a "must" for teachers. Available from publisher only.

"The Pied Piper."
ISBN: 978-0-9557881-3-0
Another play for 9–12-year-olds to act out. It's based on the original story of "The Pied Piper of Hamlyn".

"Rumpelstiltskin."
ISBN: 978-0-9557881-4-7
The adaptation of the story by that name into a play form for 9–12-year-olds. Available from publisher only.

"Christ Is My Beloved."
ISBN: 976-0-901860-84-2.
A meditation of Christ as depicted in the biblical book called "The Song of Solomon". Available from Scripture Truth Christian Publishers, Crewe, England.

"Preparation for Baptism and the Lord's Supper."
ISBN: 978-0-9557881-6-1
This book is set out as a course for Christians who wish to be baptized or to partake in the Lord's Supper. It contains

worksheets that may be photocopied for the personal use of the purchaser.

"The Epistle of Paul to the Romans." A book for Bible study.
ISBN: 978-0-9575503-1-5 Available from publisher only.

"Bursting the Bubble of Unbelief. A Bible Study Course in Ten Lessons."
ISBN: 978-0-9575503-0-8

"The Interpreter. Stories of the Prophet Daniel."
ISBN: 978-0-9575503-2-2
Stories for juniors. Illustrations in colour.

"Joseph and David and Goliath in Rhyme."
ISBN: 978-0-9575503-5-3
A book with colouring pages for children.

"A First Hymn a Day."
ISBN 978-0-9557881-7-8

"A Second Hymn a Day."
ISBN 978-0-9557881-8-5

"A Third Hymn a Day."
ISBN 978-0-9575503-9-1

"A Fourth Hymn a Day"
ISBN 978-0-9575503-9-1

"A Fifth Hymn-a-Day"
ISBN: 978-0-9575503-8-4

"A Sixth Hymn-a-Day"
ISBN: 978-0-9575503-7-7

"A Seventh Hymn-a-Day"
ISBN: 978-0-9575503-6-0 Currently available from publisher only.

These last seven books each contain 366 original hymns written by the author and complemented by quotations from the old Authorised Version of the Bible. The first six hymn-a-days six of these are also found as ebooks on Amazon.

The Quest For Life.
ISBN: 978-1-9196180-1-2
This is an adaptation of part One of Bunyan's Pilgrim's Progress. It is aimed at youngsters of nine years and older. Currently available from Mathetes Publishing only.